Saying YES to Marriage

Saying YES to Marriage

"... and the two shall become one flesh."

MARK 10:8

William H. Willimon

Judson Press ® Valley Forge

SAYING YES TO MARRIAGE

Copyright © 1979
Judson Press, Valley Forge, PA 19481

Unless otherwise indicated, Bible quotations in this volume are in accordance with the Revised Standard Version of the Bible, copyrighted 1946, 1952, 1971, 1973 © by the Division of Christian Education of the National Council of the Churches of Christ in the United States of America, and are used by permission.

Other versions of the Bible quoted in this book are:

The Holy Bible, King James Version.

The New English Bible, Copyright © The Delegates of the Oxford University Press and the Syndics of the Cambridge University Press, 1961, 1970.

Library of Congress Cataloging in Publication Data

Willimon, William H.
  Saying yes to marriage.

  Includes bibliographical references.
    1. Marriage. 2. Sexual ethics. 3. Marriage—Moral and religious aspects.   4. Sex and religion. I. Title.
HQ734.W753   301.42   79-12581
ISBN 0-8170-0812-8

The name JUDSON PRESS is registered as a trademark in the U.S. Patent Office.

Printed in the U.S.A. ✠

Since "I love you" may simply mean, in all sorts of subtle ways, "I love *me*, and want *you*," and since such love need not at all change its ulterior purpose in loving in order to want another in the same supposed interest of self-fulfillment, a person had better subject his love to this severe testing: see if he can promise permanence in love for another person precisely under those conditions, referred to in the expressions "for worse," "for poorer," and "in sickness," under which he will have to give rather than derive benefit from the marriage relationship.*

*Paul Ramsey, *Basic Christian Ethics* (New York: Charles Scribner's Sons, 1950), p. 330. Dr. Ramsey has also written a short pamphlet on a Christian view of sex within, outside, and before marriage entitled "One Flesh," published by Grove Books in England.

FOR
PATSY

Contents

Introduction

Marriage as a Subversive Activity

This book about marriage is written by a Christian minister, teacher, husband, and father. I mention my various vocations simply to alert you at the outset to some of the personal presuppositions with which I have approached this writing. I have an emotional investment in what I say here because I am writing about a human relationship from which I have derived much happiness, unhappiness, frustration, love, challenge, and growth. If you are looking for a reasoned, objective, polite discussion of marriage, you will be disappointed by this book. I hope that my own argument does not lapse into narrow-minded ax grinding, but if it does, then my only defense is to claim (with Nietzsche) that human beings ought never be reasonable, objective, or polite in discussing matters of supreme consequence.

With that warning here at the beginning, I invite you to join me in a fresh look at an old institution. Often we do not know how much something means to us until we are about to lose it. Some are of the opinion that we are about to lose marriage. We have thrown many ancient prejudices, customs, concepts, and institutions overboard in the past few years and seem to be getting along quite well without them—why not discard marriage?

Indeed, record numbers of America's people are discarding marriage, or at least raising troublesome new questions about it. In one of my last pastorates I "presided over" more divorces than marriages. Keeping account of the divorces, near divorces, trysts, breakups, and swaps often seemed like a full-time job. I increasingly found myself ministering to people in all sorts of open or clandestine "arrangements" outside of marriage. It seemed as if a time of cohabitation had replaced the traditional engagement period and varying degrees of sexual experimentation had replaced what used to be called "dating."

In 1975, the number of divorces in America exceeded one million for the first time in history. Divorces have increased every year since 1962 and have more than doubled from 1966–1975. While the number of marriages declined from 10.6 to 10 per 1,000 people from 1969 to 1975, the number of divorces in the same period climbed from 3.2 to 4.8 per 1,000 people. There does appear to be a leveling off of this rapid rise in divorces as we end the 1970s, but most statisticians feel that a high divorce rate is with us for a long time.[1] The numbers simply tell us what most of us have already experienced among our own families and friends—marriage has come upon troubled times.

At a recent worship conference in my denomination, a number of participants called upon the church to develop new rituals for "homosexual marriages" and the public union of two heterosexuals who are "committed to each other but not for a lifetime arrangement." A denominational committee has already developed experimental "Rituals with the Divorced."[2] Within the Women's Movement, a number of its leaders have charged marriage with being the very essence of female servitude. It seems as if war has been declared upon the traditional institution of Christian marriage and many in the church are ready to enlist.

Some have reacted to these attacks on marriage in the same way that the church has often reacted in other times of stress; they close their eyes to the problem, proceed as if nothing had changed, ignore marital stress and divorce when it occurs, and assume that if we just repeat all the old formulas and clichés in a loud enough voice, these new demons will go away. I do not think these troublesome demons will be exorcized either by pious pronouncements about the "sanctity of marriage" or by snuggling up to the demons and trying to baptize them by cultural accommodation.

In this book I wish to argue that instead of being an outmoded vestige of the past or a dreary relic from a sinking bourgeois culture, which we Christians must now heroically labor to keep afloat, Christian marriage has a future. It is a future that cuts to the core of our shallow, selfish, hedonistic, contemporary culture. The tensions upon marriage are merely the side effects of the sicknesses within our society as a whole. In a world gone crazy with its own self-delusions and falsehoods, Christian marriage has become a shockingly subversive activity. In a most revolutionary way, Christian marriage challenges many of the values we have sold ourselves on in the past few years and subverts some of our favorite modern myths.

I would like to thank some of my partners in this sublime subversion: the students and faculty of Duke Divinity School, my fellow pastors in the United Methodist Church in South Carolina, parishioners in my former pastorates, and, my chief fellow agitator, my wife Patsy.

Notes for the Introduction

[1] *Monthly Vital Statistics Report; Annual Summary for the United States, 1975* (Rockville, Maryland: U. S. Dept. of Health, Education, and Welfare).

[2] *Ritual in a New Day: An Invitation* (Nashville: Abingdon Press, 1976), pp. 73-96.

Her image had passed into his soul for ever and no word had broken the holy silence of his ecstasy. Her eyes had called him and his soul had leaped at the call. To live, to err, to fall, to triumph, to recreate life out of life! A wild angel had appeared to him, the angel of mortal youth and beauty, an envoy from the fair courts of life, to throw open before him in an instant of ecstasy the gates of all the ways of error and glory. On and on and on and on!*

*James Joyce, *A Portrait of the Artist as a Young Man* (New York: The Viking Press, Inc., 1964), p. 200. © 1964 by the Estate of James Joyce.

1

Sex: Gift or God?

Back in the eighth century B.C., a prophet named Hosea cried out against the sins of Israel, saying that the Lord of Israel had problems with his people. The people had forsaken their true God and their true identity and had gone lusting after a false god. The false god is named Ba'al, a Canaanite deity whom the Israelites had come to know through their pagan neighbors since moving to the Promised Land.

In a tender passage which would make any Puritan blush with its erotic imagery, the Lord is compared to a husband who has an unfaithful wife. Israel is the wife and she has gone after a lover named Ba'al. The Lord, the faithful husband, desires to woo her and win her back:

"Therefore, behold, I will allure her,
  and bring her into the wilderness,
  and speak tenderly to her.
And there I will give her her vineyards,
  and make the Valley of Achor a door of hope.
And there she shall answer me as in the days of her youth,
  as at the time when she came out of the land of Egypt.
"And in that day, says the LORD, you will call me, 'My husband,' and no longer will you call me, 'My Ba'al.' For I will remove the names of the Ba'als from her mouth, and they shall be mentioned by name no more. And I will make for you a covenant on that day with the beasts of the field, the birds of the air, and the creeping things of the ground; and I will abolish the bow, the sword, and war from the land; and I will make you lie down in safety. And I will betroth you to me for ever; I will betroth you to me in righteousness and in justice, in steadfast love, and in mercy. I will betroth you to me in faithfulness; and you shall know the LORD" (Hosea 2:14-20).

15

Now this Ba'al of which Hosea speaks was an interesting god. Ba'al was a god of nature, a fertility god. By the worship of Ba'al, it was believed that farmers could get better crops, sheepherders could get more sheep, and parents could have more offspring. Ba'al was worshiped in spectacular ways. The temples of Ba'al were filled with cult prostitutes, and one worshiped Ba'al by engaging in sex with these temple prostitutes. Human coitus was thought to have cosmic, mystical consequences. The worship of Ba'al was the worship of nature, of the creative, reproductive forces within the world. Like all nature religions, Ba'alism had a certain earthy, utilitarian, elemental appeal. The path to human fulfillment, according to true nature worshipers, lies in blending into the rhythms and patterns of the world around us, following our feelings and doing what comes naturally.

In short, Ba'al worship was worship of sex.

And this is what caused problems for the prophet Hosea. Not that Hosea had anything against sex itself. Hosea was against the idolatry, the worship of sex. It is here that this ancient prophet starts stepping on our twentieth-century toes! Many of our current problems with marriage are related to our problems with sex. In beginning our inquiry into marriage, let us start with sex.

My, how our views on sex have changed in the past few years! Before we all got "liberated," sex was one of those things which it is reasonable to suppose that nearly everyone did, but almost no one dared to talk about. The labels "Victorian" and "Puritan," whether they actually relate to the true nature of historical Victorians or Puritans, have come to signify our former carefully suppressed dealings with sex.

The comedian Bill Cosby said that, when he was young, his father always encouraged him to talk over any questions or problems with him. Attempting to obey his father, one evening at the dinner table young Cosby asked him, "Dad, where do babies come from?" Cosby's father got up from the table, took his son into another room, sat him down, and said, "If I ever hear you talk like that again, I'll give you a spanking that you won't forget."

Particularly in the context of religion, the very mention of sex was a taboo. A minister friend of mine recalls the time when, as he was greeting his parishioners after church one Sunday, a little girl ran up and said, "Pastor, we are so excited. Our cat just had five babies yesterday." The little girl's horrified mother grabbed her daughter and pushed her away, saying, "Oh, Pastor, I can't imagine where she has learned to talk like that. We certainly don't talk about that kind of thing at home!"

We must honestly confess that the Christian church has a poor record in its historical dealings with sex. For centuries, the biblical witness notwithstanding, we regarded sex as a necessary evil. In its earliest days, the church did fight the notion that sex was evil in itself. But even marriage was a bit suspect and celibacy was considered the highest state of human existence. There has always been a tendency among Christians to value spiritual things over physical things. In spite of the fact that "the Word became flesh" in the incarnation, in spite of the fact that the New Testament never speaks of the immortality of soul or spirit, only the resurrection of the body, and in spite of Jesus' teachings about the proper use of all God's gifts, material and spiritual, we later Christians rarely mention money, politics, jobs, or sex as having any great consequence for the living of a Christian life. Of course, by neatly separating our world into dualistic physical and spiritual spheres, it is easier to live the faith. We can keep our religion "pure" by focusing only on spiritual matters and run our business, spend our money, cast our ballots, and have sex as we want to! Such separation may make life less complicated. Whether it will make it more Christian is another matter.

The perverted notion that sex is inherently evil has many sources. In part, it is the result of the Platonic dualism which influenced Hellenistic philosophy which in turn influenced the earliest Christian theology. Dualism says that the world is divided between the physical and spiritual. The physical is bad. The spiritual is good. The Gnostics, an early Christian heretical group, building upon philosophical dualism, put forth the belief that all sexual experiences, including procreation within marriage, were evil because they all participated in the evil of the material world. To support their views, Gnostics cited such biblical passages as Luke 14 where a man missed the great banquet because he married a wife!

It was in this atmosphere of Gnostic dualism, pagan libertarianism, and general indifference to the ethical demands of marriage that the church was forced to work out its own theology of marriage. Not all of its efforts were noteworthy. In the second century, Clement of Alexandria defended marriage not so much from Scripture as from Greek and Roman philosophies of natural law. Why would nature give us sex organs if sex was evil? Whenever sex is used for procreation—the "natural" purpose of marriage—it is good. Clement's natural law argument limits the purpose of sex and of marriage, but at least it raises marriage and sex from the level of absolute negatives to the status of a carefully qualified good. Not all church fathers were convinced. Gregory of Nyssa called marriage a "sad tragedy." Ambrose termed it a "galling burden," and Jerome thought the main value of marriage was that it was helpful in producing future virgins![1]

Some of the blame for our later Christian prudishness must be laid at the feet of the venerable Saint Augustine. Before his conversion, Augustine lived a rather sensual life with a mistress by whom he fathered a child. Augustine's guilt over his youthful wild oats may have influenced his rather disparaging remarks about sex and marriage. The bishop's theologically and biblically absurd proposition that sexual intercourse transmitted original sin was to degrade sex for over a thousand years.

The extremist idea that sex was the source of sin was kept alive by later fringe movements within Christianity, such as the Cathari (who taught that since Adam and Eve's invention of sexual intercourse, everything has gone downhill for the human race) and the Shakers (founded by Ann Lee who, after a difficult experience in childbirth, decided that marriage was a "covenant with death, and an agreement with hell" because marriage usually means sex). Needless to say, such extreme positions not only raised serious theological problems but also insured the rapid demise of these splinter groups. Total abstinence from sex did not encourage the production of future Cathari or Shakers!

The church as a whole weathered the storms of such extremism and dualistic condemnation of human sexuality. But, until the Protestant Reformation, marriage suffered a distinctly second-class status, and sex itself continued to be held suspect. In recent years we have come to realize how unbiblical these negative views of sex are. Genesis says that sexuality is God's idea. God created us, male and female, in his own image (Genesis 1:27) and called this arrangement "good" (Genesis 1:31). God commanded us to "be fruitful and multiply" which is a difficult commandment to obey without engaging in sex. Any sinfulness in our sexuality is not due to the way we were created but to the way we use the creation.

The Bible itself is not squeamish on the subject of sex. The Song of Solomon is an unabashed love poem which praises the joys of erotic love. A young man speaks to his beloved:

> Behold, you are beautiful, my love,
>   behold, you are beautiful!
> Your eyes are doves
>   behind your veil.
> Your hair is like a flock of goats,
>   moving down the slopes of Gilead.
> Your teeth are like a flock of shorn ewes
>   that have come up from the washing,
> all of which bear twins,
>   and not one among them is bereaved.
> Your lips are like a scarlet thread,
>   and your mouth is lovely.
> Your cheeks are like halves of a pomegranate
>   behind your veil.
> Your neck is like the tower of David,
>   built for an arsenal,
> whereon hang a thousand bucklers,
>   all of them shields of warriors.
> Your two breasts are like two fawns,
>   twins of a gazelle,
>   that feed among the lilies.
> Until the day breathes
>   and the shadows flee,
> I will hie me to the mountain of myrrh
>   and the hill of frankincense.
> —Song of Solomon 4:1-6

And his lover replies:

> My beloved is all radiant and ruddy,
>   distinguished among ten thousand.
> His head is the finest gold;
>   his locks are wavy,
>   black as a raven.
> His eyes are like doves
>   beside springs of water,
> bathed in milk,
>   fitly set.
> His cheeks are like beds of spices,
>   yielding fragrance.
> His lips are lilies,
>   distilling liquid myrrh.
> His arms are rounded gold,
>   set with jewels.
> His body is ivory work,
>   encrusted with sapphires.
> His legs are alabaster columns,

> set upon bases of gold.
> His appearance is like Lebanon,
> choice as the cedars.
> —Song of Solomon 5:10-15

This sort of thing continues until, in an overwhelming surge of passion, the youth can stand it no more and declares (7:7-8*a*):

> You are stately as a palm tree,
> and your breasts are like its clusters.
> I say I will climb the palm tree,
> and lay hold of its branches.

For centuries the church has tried to allegorize away this X-rated book of the Bible into religious respectability. But it cannot. Song of Solomon is the only book of the Bible that never mentions God. It stands there simply as a joyful, exuberant celebration of the gifts of love and sex. Anyone who thinks the Judeo-Christian faith is just for little old ladies and starched-collared old men should read the Bible! The *whole* Bible.

Thus we see that it is unbiblical, even unchristian, to regard sex itself as a sin. There is no denying that sex is seen in the Bible as a potentially troublesome and frequently abused gift of God. But it is always a gift. It is not a God, as Hosea reminds us, but nevertheless it is a divine gift. And God does not give evil gifts.

I think that bit of information (that sex is not inherently evil) has been heard by most people today. We have learned that sex is OK. It is OK to enjoy it, do it, talk about it, read about it, get better at it. Dr. Freud told us long ago to rid ourselves of our hangups over sex—so we have. In the past few years we have witnessed some rather dramatic changes in our attitudes and expressions of sexuality. I contend that some of these changes have been less than helpful.

We have exchanged the perversion of acting as if sex did not exist for an equally perverted obsession with sex. Sexual expression rather than sexual repression has become our new dogma. The psychologist Rollo May declares that we put "more emphasis on sex than any society since that of ancient Rome."[2] From our previous treatment of sex as an unmentionable we have shifted to a point at which it seems as if we have no other topic of conversation except sex. Like giggling adolescents on a perpetual pajama party, sex dominates our speech. T.V. soap operas dish up a steady diet of extramarital affairs, trysts, rendezvous, impotence, frigidity, sodomy, incest, and any other conceivable form of sexual expression. T.V. doctors, such as Dr.

Gannon and Dr. Welby, labor against what seems to be a veritable epidemic of sexual disorders. Toothpaste, which was once content to keep our teeth from rotting out, now claims to produce "sex appeal." Barbara Walters interviews the new president and his wife and asks the main question about our chief executive that all America is waiting for: "Do you sleep in the same bed?" O Ba'al, great god of sex, giver of all pleasures and good feelings, how we love you, how we worship you, whether watching your disciples cavort on our movie screens, or singing your throbbing hymns on radio's Top Forty hits, or celebrating your glory in weekend motel rituals. Ba'al worship is alive and well! Praise Sex, from whom all blessings flow! Hosea, where are you now that we need you?

Of course, Ba'al did not win our hearts overnight. What we see blossoming about us today took a few years of cultivation. Rollo May lays the blame for much of this erotic frenzy upon the shoulders of that Viennese father of psychoanalysis, Sigmund Freud. Dr. Freud was one of the few Victorians who *did* talk about sex. Freud traced many forms of neurosis to our old unhealthy suppression of our sexuality. Sex is an integral part of our humanity. To deny it or feel that it is dirty or evil is to risk serious psychological consequences.

But Freud, or should I say our popular interpretations and misinterpretations of Freud, said more than this. By the 1920s, the Freudian mythology of human sexuality was part of the average person's world view. The satirist, Tom Wolfe, has described this Freudian view of humanity as "Man, the Boiler Room."[3] Somewhat crudely restated, Freud described the *libido* or sexual "energy" as a kind of pressure analogous to steam which builds up in a closed system to a point at which it demands release. Human sexuality is thus conceived of as a steam boiler which must be regularly released (preferably in the form of an exuberant, shuddering, earth-shaking, guilt-free orgasm) if one is to maintain a healthy psyche. If not released, all sorts of psychological maladies are said to result.

It is Wolfe's opinion that Freud's image of the human being as a sexual boiler room animates today's sexual revolution. Drs. Reuben (*Everything You Always Wanted to Know About Sex*) and Comfort (*The Joy of Sex*) and Madame Hollander (*The Happy Hooker*) tell us to heal ourselves by letting the steam out. Even some women's liberation theorists, who readily criticize Freud as the perpetrator of our most sinister male-dominated myths, press the boiler-room axiom on their sisters, telling them to take the sexual initiative, masturbate, mechanically vibrate, liberate the *libido*, and let the steam out!

Who can blame any red-blooded adolescent for not wanting to clog up his or her natural sexual energy by obeying stuffy parental injunctions against back-seat sex? We seem to live by D. H. Lawrence's proposal that mutual orgasm should be the supreme goal of civilization! Pornographers, using the boiler-room theory, now argue that they are society's "safety valve"—claiming that the potential rapist or child molester discharges his or her *libido* in more socially acceptable ways in their peep shows, skin flicks, and porn magazines. The editors of such magazines as *Hustler* parade as social workers! They say their magazines help us to clean our valves and pipes and thus keep our boilers from bursting. A massage parlor operator tells a T.V. interviewer, "We help save marriages, because a man can come in here and get what he needs when he can't get it at home." Swinging, group sex, bestiality, bisexuality, etc., have become necessary aspects of good mental hygiene!

Wolfe notes one serious problem with Freud's boiler-room myth— there is not one shred of empirical evidence to support it. In this age of neurophysiology, when we are now able to study the working of the brain and central nervous system through electrode implants, etc., no buildups of "pressure" or "energy," sexual or otherwise, have been located. Neurophysiological studies suggest that the brain is more like an electronic circuit, a computer rather than a steam boiler. Human behavior is determined, not by periodic pressure blowouts, but rather by which lines are open and which messages get through.

Using this analogy of the electrical circuit or computer, such pastimes as pornography are seen not as safety valves but rather as input into the system. This input tends to open certain gates, close out others, and determines the operation of the entire "circuit." Thus we must ask, "Is pornography the effect of our sexual problems or the cause of them?"[4] Whether our sexual behavior is healthy or not depends not on how much steam is released, but rather upon the more difficult questions of the nature of the input, the end results of the behavior, the relationship of the input to the total operation of the system, and other such factors. Perhaps what makes the human sexual response truly *human* is the ability to decide when, where, with whom, and in what form it will take place.

Of course, comparing a human being to a computer may strike you as being even more simplistic and dehumanizing than Freud's steam boiler. The computer analogy tends to be as reductionistic in overemphasizing the cognitive as Freud's reductionistic overemphasis of the biological as the basis for human behavior. But at least this analogy has the advantage of the possibility of empirical verification or rejection. It suggests that Freud, his psychoanalytic heirs, and the folk wisdom of modern "liberated" sexual enthusiasts may have little more to offer us toward the understanding of the complexities of human sexuality than the wisdom that can be gleaned from the conversation in a junior high boys' rest room.

Another contemporary expression of sexuality is the appearance of the marriage (sex) manual.

The marriage manuals tell us that performance is the key to successful sexuality. With Dr. Comfort's book in hand, through certain bedroom gymnastics and erotic contortions, it is said that any couple can achieve the orgasmic fulfillment they desire. Rollo May observes that the marriage manuals have shifted the burden on women from the older question of "Will she or won't she?" to the performance question of "Can she or can't she?" The challenge has thus shifted from a concern over one's sexual morals to a preoccupation with one's sexual adequacy.[5] This can have devastating results. Marriage counselors have reported "an increase in the number of married women troubled by a lack of orgasmic fulfillment and by husbands who expect fantasies adopted from popular magazines to be reenacted in their own bedroom."[6] Otherwise intelligent people become convinced that they are suffering from some form of sexual dysfunction (which is actually a rarity) when they simply suffer from unrealistic images and expectations of what sex should be like.

In our sex-saturated paganism, everybody is talking to everybody else about sex. Pop magazines have told us that sex is better on the tops of office desks, in subway cars, and in phone booths. Our youth tell us that sex is simply a good way of getting to know someone, recreation with no strings attached. Radical women's liberationists tell us that sex is a tool of male power which is used to make women into dependent sexual objects and unthinking sex toys. Marriage manuals tell us that sex is related to double-jointed calisthenics.

Like our popular acceptance of the steam-boiler analogy, many of us have unquestioningly bought into these contemporary notions of human sexuality. We should at least inquire how these notions about sex will affect our images of ourselves, our relationships with one another, the future of our society, and (some may even be so bold as to ask) our relationship with God. Whereas we have criticized the older dualists for separating the flesh from the soul and the material from the spiritual, many of us have fallen into the same error from the other side. The older dualists treated our spirits apart from our bodies. The new dualists would focus upon our bodies to the exclusion of our spirits. Or, more to the point, they assume that sex is an independent human activity which can be practiced apart from any consideration of our human values, intellects, and ultimate strivings.

Frederick Buechner admits that it is appealing to think that adultery, promiscuity, masturbation, swinging, swapping, etc., are permissible "as long as nobody gets hurt," as long as we are simply cleaning out our plumbing and "nothing else."

> The trouble is that human beings are so hopelessly psychosomatic in composition that whatever happens to the *soma* [body] happens also to the *psyche* [spirit], and vice versa.
> . . . who is to say who gets hurt and who does not? Maybe the injuries are all internal. . . . Maybe the only person who gets hurt is you.[7]

Human beings do not live only by their genitals. They live also by their minds and hearts. The new dualists would rip sex out of the context of total human existence. This can be done only at the peril of dividing ourselves against ourselves, cutting us off from others and from our true selves.[8]

At least, this is what the Christian faith, at its best, has traditionally said about sex. Having heard the old and the new prophets of Ba'al and the old and the new dualists, let us now examine in more detail what the faith has said about sex.

Notes for Chapter 1

[1] Jacob Dominian, *Christian Marriage* (London: Darton, Longman, and Todd Ltd., 1968), pp. 26-27.

[2] Rollo May, *Love and Will* (New York: W. W. Norton & Co., Inc., 1969), p. 39.

[3] Tom Wolfe, *Mauve Gloves & Madmen, Clutter & Vine* (New York: Farrar, Straus & Giroux, Inc., 1976).

⁴For an empirical study of the complexities of the cause-effect question, see Michael J. Goldstein and Harold S. Kant, *Pornography and Sexual Deviance* (Berkeley: University of California Press, 1973), chap. 11.

⁵May, *op. cit.,* pp. 43-45. As an example of what May is talking about, see Georgia Kline-Graber and Benjamin Graber's *Women's Orgasm: A Guide to Sexual Satisfaction* (New York: Bobbs-Merrill Co., Inc., 1975). The authors cite ominous consequences for women who fail to achieve regular orgasm—self-induced or in intercourse.

⁶"Till Divorce Do Us Part," *Maclean's* (April 19, 1976), pp. 28-29.

⁷Frederick Buechner, *Wishful Thinking: A Theological ABC* (New York: Harper & Row, Publishers, 1973), pp. 87-88.

⁸It is interesting to hear a secular psychiatrist plead for a change in focus from our current "technical-anatomical" view of sex to a more "spiritual-psychological" approach. Complaining that modern sexual liberation has led to an actual diminution of sex, Dr. Robertiello says, "People have somehow forgotten that sex—the essence of sexuality—always has been and still is in the mind. Passion is still not anatomical" (Richard C. Robertiello, "The Decline and Fall of Sex," *The Journal of Sex Research*, vol. 12, no. 1 [February, 1976], pp. 70-73).

The Ragged Wood

O hurry where by water among the trees
The delicate stepping stag and his lady sigh
When they have but looked upon their images,
Would none had ever loved but you and I!

Or have you heard that sliding silver-shoed,
Pale silver-proud queen-woman of the sky,
When the sun looked out of his golden hood:
O that none ever loved but you and I!

O hurry to the ragged wood, for there
I will drive all those lovers out and cry—
O my share of the world, O yellow hair,
No one has ever loved but you and I!*

*Reprinted with permission of Macmillan Publishing Co., Inc., from *Collected Poems* by William Butler Yeats. © 1924 by Macmillan Publishing Co., Inc., renewed 1952 by Bertha Georgie Yeats.

2

Sex: A Christian View

Earlier we noted the rather poor record the Christian church has had in its dealings with human sexuality. Contrary to the teaching of Augustine *et alia*, we now know that it is unbiblical to think that sex is inherently sinful. Sex is a gift. Having gotten that bit of information across, we must now challenge some of the cherished assumptions of today's sexual revolution and say that, in spite of the pronouncements of contemporary prophets of Ba'al, sex is not God. There is demonic potential within the gift of sex when that gift is improperly used. Or, as Frederick Buechner puts it: "Contrary to Mrs. Grundy, sex is not sin. Contrary to Hugh Hefner, it's not salvation either. Like nitroglycerin, it can be used either to blow up bridges or heal hearts."[1]

The faith has traditionally said that there are three wrong ways to view our sexuality: we are not to idolize sex, or sacramentalize sex, or trivialize sex.[2]

First, we are not to idolize sex. Martin Luther said that whatever you give your money to, whatever you praise the loudest, whatever you would sacrifice your daughter for—that is your god. Or, as Paul Tillich put it, your god is what ultimately concerns you. Your god is what you love the most. For many of us, sex has become idolatry as surely as those ancient Israelites bowed down before Ba'al. The playboy philosophy of self-centered, detached hedonism, the frantic search for bigger and better orgasms and for someone else to "score" with: this is putting sex in place of God—and it is a false god.

Sexual expertise is not the mark of a good person. The Miss

27

America, Miss World, Miss Universe pageants—those yearly celebrations of shapely femaleness—glorify the most shallow, superficial aspects of women. And mere machismo on a mattress does not make a true man. Our deepest human needs will not be solved by sex. Our common humanity will not be enhanced by improving our sexual techniques. Our sexual identity—be it heterosexual, homosexual, or bisexual—is not our most basic identity. Sex is not God. It will not give us that which we most need and for which we most desperately search.

Sex is a deeply significant unitive act in the Bible. But, contrary to the often mushy, erotic mysticism of poets like Kahlil Gibran and D. H. Lawrence, sex is never regarded as a mystical or revelatory act in the Bible. Israel was surrounded by people who practiced fertility rites, cultic prostitution, and magical attempts to induce nature's production through human sex acts. These acts and their supporting theology are specifically rejected in the Old Testament (see Hosea 2:2-13; Amos 2:7-8). The sex act is not, in itself, a specifically religious or edifying experience and it reveals little about the ultimate truth of the universe. Sex is a gift of God. It is not God.

A second wrong way to look at sex, related to the first, is to sacramentalize it. The church has traditionally defined such sacraments as the Lord's Supper and baptism as "means of grace." Sacraments, by their nature, convey God's grace to us in visible, tangible ways. Sex is not holy, extraordinary, or divine. The Bible does not speak of sex as a sacrament. While the Roman Catholic Church regards marriage as a sacrament, we Protestants do not. Luther and Calvin both rejected the idea that marriage and, by implication, sex are special channels of divine grace.[3]

We human beings are male and female but, more importantly, we are human beings. While our sexual differences are significant, they are not ultimately significant. As Paul told us: "There is neither Jew nor Greek, there is neither slave nor free, there is neither male nor female; for you are all one in Christ Jesus" (Galatians 3:28). The basis for our human dignity and self-worth lies not in our vauntful attempts to claim our special glory as women or men, "straight" or "gay." The source of our true dignity and worth lies in our unity with the One who yoked himself in solidarity with us and thus bestowed true value upon us all as God's children—Jesus the Christ.

One regrettable consequence of our current preoccupation with sex is that many people in our midst feel excluded or freakish because sex is not their overall concern in life. The church has always affirmed that one can serve God and humanity whether one is unmarried or married. My own life would have been impoverished had it not been for the great influence of unmarried schoolteachers, Scout leaders, professors, and friends upon my personal development. I doubt if they could have given me as much of their time, love, and affection if they had been pressed by the responsibilities of married life. There are other ways to express and receive love besides sex. The church needs to say this again in loud and clear terms.

Sex is a delightful gift of God to be used and enjoyed, but sex, by itself, will not save, heal, edify, or convey grace. For verification of this, one need only consider our current sexual dilemma. Technology and modern mores with their birth-control pills, illustrated sex manuals, and liberated sexual behavior have contributed to our physical pleasure and knowledge of sexuality. But has our emotional satisfaction increased proportionally? The more uninhibited we have become in our sexual expression, the more we have realized the limits of sex alone to help us. Sex is not a sacrament.

Finally, we are not to trivialize sex. Sex is more than exercise, more than recreation. The "playboy philosophy" of sex is wrong, not because it thinks too much of sex, but because it does not take sex seriously enough. Psychotherapists have long noted our tendency to trivialize and reduce those things which threaten us the most. Thus, our great fear of death leads us to avoid confronting death by speaking of death in veiled euphemisms ("passed on," "gone on to his reward," etc.) or to feign a lightheartedness by joking about death. We invent new words and cute jokes in an attempt to overcome our uncomfortableness with this threatening fact of life.

Along with death, sex has traditionally been the other major threatening and uncomfortable human experience. Thus we have invented euphemistic expressions and cute slang words to label our genitals and sex acts. It is no mystery why the "dirty joke" is the stock and trade of the average adolescent. Adolescence brings on fears and worries about one's sexuality. By joking about it, sex is reduced to more manageable size. Sex becomes just a game in which the goal is to "score" with someone else. For many people, sex has been whittled down to mere recreation, "It's just a game. It doesn't matter with whom you play the game as long as you have fun for now."

The Judeo-Christian tradition takes sex more seriously. It speaks of sex as one of the deepest, most emotional, most costly, most fulfilling, and most dangerous encounters that can take place between two human beings. There is no denying that the Bible appears ambivalent on the nature of sex. Along with the continuing affirmation that sex, as a part of God's creation, is "very good," there are the seemingly contradictory laws, admonitions, and strict pronouncements that carefully limit the practice of sex and impose harsh penalties for those who engage in illicit sex (for instance, see Genesis 2:25; Proverbs 31:3). The reason for this apparent ambivalence is simply that the Bible says that sex, because of its very power and creativity, can be self-destructive and demonic when abused. "Like nitroglycerin, it can be used either to blow up bridges or heal hearts."[4]

This is probably why Jesus uttered that rather stern remark, ". . . every one who looks at a woman lustfully has already committed adultery with her in his heart" (Matthew 5:28). Here Jesus is pointing out that in lust, as in adultery, the intended purpose of sex—the union of a man and woman in the most intimate of relationships—is thwarted by reducing the other person into an object to be used (and thus abused) for one's own self-satisfaction. Jesus here goes on record against making a male or female into a "sex object." Clearly for Jesus, sex is more than the mere physical merging of two bodies. Intentions, motives, and human results enter into judgments about sex.

By the way, it should be noted that in this passage on "adultery of the heart," Jesus was definitely not condemning the natural, transitory sexual desire that every person feels for other people on frequent occasions. He was simply noting the detrimental consequences of prolonged desire for another person who is not one's legitimate (he uses the term "adultery") partner. There is no condemnation of proper sexual expression intended here.[5]

Paul has often been accused of having a negative view of sex and of being an advocate of Christian celibacy. But a close reading of Paul's most extensive treatment of sexuality, 1 Corinthians 6–7, shows that, far from disparaging sex, he is urging the right use of sex as a creation of a loving God. To the Corinthians, who lived in a culture where cult prostitution was widely practiced, Paul condemns such sexual travesties as transitory encounters with prostitutes because they destroy the unitive function for which sex was created. The body was the very "temple of the Holy Spirit" for Paul. To defile that temple through the abuse of one of God's greatest gifts is the sin Paul condemns. The abuse of sex and not sex itself is the source of the sin.

While 1 Corinthians 7 is often cited as evidence that Paul had a distinctly anti-sex, anti-marriage bias, consideration of the passage as a whole shows Paul's traditional Jewish view of sex and marriage as good gifts of God. He here forbids married people to become single. To those who are single his advice not to marry is a result of Paul's belief that he lived in the end time and the world would shortly pass away.[6] Nowhere does Paul imply that singleness is a superior moral state or that there is any inherent evil in sex or marriage. In fact, he warns married couples, "Do not deny yourselves to one another . . ." (1 Corinthians 7:5a, NEB). Paul is hardly an ascetic.

Jesus and Paul were simply saying that sex is a complex phenomenon, with far-reaching consequences for one's whole being and all of one's relationships with other people. As Freud discovered, we are sexual beings from the time of our birth and will be, in one form or another, sexual beings until we die. For every person who has found the "joy of sex," there are others who have been emotionally, spiritually, or physically destroyed by the ravages of abused sex. While the Christian faith does not idolize or sacramentalize sex, it does take sex very seriously—much more seriously than many of those who now proclaim and practice their newfound sexual "freedom." Sex is not to be trivialized.

By saying what sex is not, I hope we have said, in some sense, what sex is. The primary purpose of sex according to Genesis, and to Jesus who quotes Genesis, is to bring about a union of two people. "The two shall become one flesh. So they are no longer two but one flesh. What therefore God has joined together, let not man put asunder" (Mark 10:8-9; Genesis 2:24). The function of sex is to unite. The Old Testament speaks of sexual intercourse as "knowing" (Genesis 4:1; 1 Samuel 1:19-20), as a path to the deepest and most revealing intimacy that can be realized among men and women.

The modern world has attempted to degrade human sexual relations to the level of animalistic copulation. Intercourse is called "screwing" in an attempt to dehumanize and depersonalize this mysterious sexual "knowing." When Paul speaks of the human mating act, he calls it a *musterion*, a "mystery" (Ephesians 5:32). It is a mysterious event, a meeting that is symbolic of the deepest, most penetrating of all human encounters. Human sexuality, when it is practiced as God created it to be, is *union* and not orgasmic release or groaning catharsis. It is no accident that the current pop literature on sex tends to stress orgasm over union. This keeps our sex neatly detached from our total personalities, keeps it self-centered and mechanical. But truly to enter not only the body but also the life of another is to participate in a human mystery no more or less greater than the divine mystery of God entering creation and becoming one with it. Our God is a God who constantly works for union and calls us to do the same. Sex is one God-given means of working toward this loving union with others.

When it is all said and done, we should probably not take today's sexual revolution with too much seriousness. Much of our present "revolution" in sex is just the short-lived and superficial outburst of a bunch of neo-Puritans who think we have been liberated in the past few years and now frantically rush about for something to do with our liberation. We are much like those ancient Israelites who finally got liberated in the Promised Land after slavery in Egypt, only to become enslaved to their own selfish desires, their neighbor's pagan idols, and their rather adolescent view of the world. The worship of Ba'al must have been fun for a while. But those ancient sons and daughters of Israel found that you cannot keep it up forever. Reality rushes in, playboys and playgirls inevitably get old and get wrinkles, and the false god tends to take more from us (our families, our values, our brains, our dignity) than he gives back. The ecstasy of sex lasts only for a few minutes and then it's over. But that is usually always the way with false gods.

Sex is important but not ultimately important. It is a gift and not a god. It will not free us, completely fulfill us, or ultimately satisfy us. There is only One who can do that for us—and you know His name already.

Notes for Chapter 2

[1] Frederick Buechner, *Wishful Thinking* (New York: Harper & Row, Publishers, 1973), p. 87.

[2] These three aspects were suggested in an article, "Human Sexuality," *Response* (January, 1976), pp. 18-21.

[3] Jacob Dominian, *Christian Marriage: the Challenge of Change* (London: Darton, Longman & Todd Ltd., 1968), p. 33.

[4] Buechner, *op. cit.,* p. 87.

[5] Stephen Sapp, "Biblical Perspectives on Human Sexuality," *The Duke Divinity School Review,* vol. 41, no. 2 (Spring, 1976), pp. 115-116.

[6] *Ibid.,* pp. 119-121.

Dedication to My Wife

To whom I owe the leaping delight
That quickens my senses in our wakingtime
And the rhythm that governs the response of our sleepingtime,
    The breathing in unison

Of lovers whose bodies smell of each other
Who think the same thoughts without need of speech
And babble the same speech without need of meaning.

No peevish winter wind shall chill
No sullen tropic sun shall wither
The roses in the rose-garden which is ours and ours only

But this dedication is for others to read:
These are private words addressed to you in public.*

3

Old Pagans and New Playmates

It was predictable that marriage would become a focal point of revolt during the revolutionary sixties. To subvert the time-honored institution of marriage, to call its values and customs into question, or to uncover marriage as a tool of an oppressive society was seen as an attack upon the very core of decadent "bourgeois morality." The hypocrisy of many marriages, the stifling drabness of many marriages, and the tragic enslavement of women in many marriages were cited as evidence that marriage had had its day. The sixties and seventies were marked by the deaths of a number of American institutions: the "Jim Crow" laws of racial segregation, the military draft, America's role as "policeman" for the world, the all-male Little League Baseball team; now, marriage seemed to be on the way out.

Many of the criticisms of marriage and its attendant mores were valid. For Christians (or any other thinking persons) to ignore or defend these weaknesses is unpardonable. This book will not attempt to brush aside the difficulties of marriage in our modern world or to deny that the institution of marriage is frequently abused by the actual marriages of some of its most ardent defenders. What this book will attempt to say about Christian marriage is an echo of Martin Luther's principle for the reform of Christian worship—*abusus non tollit usum*—"abuse of a custom does not necessarily mean that the custom itself is bad and should be stopped." Marriage has come upon rough times because these are generally rough times for living and loving whether one is married or not. Some of today's "revolutionaries" who hope to hasten the demise of our many "sick institutions" should be reminded that some of the institutions themselves may be sound and are simply suffering from various infections brought on by a generally sick society.

While it may be overly dramatic to speak of an "attack" on marriage, who would deny that marriage has been severely criticized and challenged in the past few years? As usual, the movies mirror what most of us are thinking and some of us are doing. After decades of idealizing marriage in pop culture's Doris Day and Rock Hudson movies where boy meets girl, marries girl, and then beds girl somewhere in suburban bliss in Scarsdale where they have children and are happy ever after, movies now inundate us with efforts to debunk marriage. *The Graduate* was billed as a "courageous" commentary on today's youth who brave society's hypocritical conventions and seek happiness in spite of all those time-honored myths about marriage. In a climactic scene, the graduate rushes into the church, rescues his love from the clutches of a clean-cut young man and his ecclesiastical collaborators, disrupts their wedding, sweeps the grateful bride away, battles the outraged wedding party at the rear door of the church, locks them all kicking and screaming inside the church, and flees with his love. From *The Graduate* we were treated to a steady flow of "courageous" young men and women who escaped not only the marital ceremony but also monogamy altogether in order to experience "true love." From there, things went downhill (as they usually do in the mediocrity of our mass media) until avoiding matrimony, thumbing our illicit noses, and "doing our own thing" in the buff on the silver screen were no longer "courageous"—these were simply the conventional movie-TV-magazine things to do. The Doris Day-Rock Hudson sentimental absurdities of the fifties were exchanged for Kristofferson-Streisand sentimental (albeit sensual) absurdities of the seventies. The female pensioners sleeping with teenagers (*Harold and Maude*) and erudite professors sleeping with drop-out students (*What's Up, Doc?*) tell us that we really haven't come all that far in our quest for *cinema verité*. Whereas marriage used to be portrayed as the magic formula which solved all personality differences and eradicated all practical problems as "they lived happily ever after," now sex (preferably extramarital) is portrayed as having the same miraculous effects.

While the foes of traditional monogamy assume many guises and advance various arguments against marriage, let me focus upon those things which I consider to be the major challenges.

The first contemporary challenge to marriage is not so much a specific alternative as a general state of mind (and body) which underlies most of the other alternatives to marriage—the new hedonism. Hedonism, as a philosophy and as a life-style, has had a long, if not distinguished, history. For the classical pagan hedonist, pleasure is the guiding principle of life. Hedonism has taken a number of forms over the centuries. The Cyrenaics felt that the only attainable good for humanity was the sentient pleasure of the moment. Therefore the goal of life is to crowd as much enjoyment as possible into each moment. You only go around once; so live it up while you are here. While the Epicureans agreed that pleasure is life's supreme goal, they added that reason should guide us in our pursuit of pleasure. Self-control over our choice of pleasures is indispensable in order to keep pain, said to be the antithesis of pleasure, to a minimum.

In the eighteenth century, Jeremy Bentham revived hedonism as a moral theory. Morality, for Bentham, was reducible to the simple formula that each person should seek his or her own greatest pleasure. This led to a refined type of utilitarianism—whatever "works" to produce our pleasure is right and good. Joseph Butler effectively attacked Bentham's utilitarianism, suggesting that pleasure is never a suitable good since pleasure comes only as a by-product or bonus when our desires get their way. Attention should be focused upon the appropriateness of our desires and their objects rather than upon the possibility of subsequent pleasures. Admittedly, hedonists have often suffered a bad press at the hands of their detractors. The "pleasure" which the hedonist seeks is not always purely physical pleasure, and most classical hedonists taught that physical pleasure is "lower" pleasure which is inevitably ephemeral and often attended by pain.

Hedonism is always at the core of pragmatic and utilitarian approaches to life. It has the appeal of a simple, uncomplicated view of human existence. For the hedonist, all thorny questions of ethics and morality can be solved by the simple question, "Does it make *me* feel good?" And yet, life is neither simple nor uncomplicated. Even in our most base and animalistic simplicity, we humans are engaged in something more than a mere pursuit of pleasure and avoidance of pain. What causes us pain and what causes us pleasure may be very different kinds of things. And a system of ethics which is based on gross self-interest hardly seems to be "ethical" to anyone.

The new hedonism shares many of the weaknesses of the old hedonism along with the usual superficiality and commercial excess that underlie many other facets of contemporary life. The new hedonists are fond of thinking of themselves as the avant-garde, as courageous revolutionaries who are turning a stuffy old society upside down. And yet, as one examines the rhetoric and the results of the current revolt against marriage, the first thing one notices is its failure to be truly revolutionary. To be revolutionary is to be radical, to cut to the root (latin: *radix* = "root") of a society. But the "revolt" against marriage does not really overturn anything. Indeed, it seems only to accentuate and perpetuate the very worst elements of twentieth-century Western culture.

The so-called revolution against marriage is no revolution. It is merely one more example of our modern Western craving for instant gratification. We want everything right away, without risk, involvement, or investment—from instant oatmeal to instant sex. We are a society of instant hedonists. The pursuit of pleasure, companionship, emotional highs, and sexual joys for their own sakes is in fact an unconscious collaboration with "the system" at its worst rather than a rejection of the system. Immediate gratification is the fundamental value that sustains the dream world of advertising. Advertisers are constantly telling us that we can have what we dream of and we can have it *now* if we just smoke this, swallow this, or smear this under our arms or on our faces. Sex is predominant in advertising because it is so successful in selling the magic potions that promise to give us what we want (popularity, immortality, happiness, pleasure, perpetual youth, and the like).

The "revolt" against marriage serves only to reinforce the inhumane values that lie at the heart of the worst excesses of our capitalistic consumption-oriented system. We live in a throw-away economy in which waste is a virtual necessity to keep production and consumption feeding one another. Things must be thrown away in order to make room for the new and improved model. In such a system, carried to its logical extreme, not only every *thing* but also every *person* seems expendable. The need for labor (people) is controlled merely by the law of supply and demand. People are of value only as long as they are useful in helping us to get what we want. Sex becomes recreation, quick gratification with no messy leftovers. Marriage becomes problematic in such a system because what do you do when you have gotten all the pleasure—be it intellectual, sexual, economic, or emotional pleasure—out of another person?

"Do Your Own Thing" is an appropriate slogan for the new hedonists. A survey of *Playboy* magazine over the past ten years reveals the end result of our sexual "revolution." In the mid-sixties, the typical *Playboy* short story sex fantasy portrayed a James Bond type sexual encounter in which hyper-male, working with seductively sexy female, finally seduces her half-willing little body into a marvelous "experience." By the late sixties, there were more stories in which hyper-male meets widely erotic female playmate on a deserted beach or in an art museum; they lock together in a rough and tumble frenzy of "lovemaking" and part without exchanging names, addresses, or many words beyond the requisite grunts and groans. In the early seventies, stories of homosexual couplings made the *Playboy* scene. Heterosexual love merely complicates the situation. "Doing your own thing" with your own kind is easier. Finally, in the mid-seventies, the *Playboy* literary fantasies began extolling the joys of masturbation—love by oneself. Here we see the end result of a process begun some time ago. Since pleasure comes from aggressively seeking one's best self-interests, love is best without the troublesome assistance of another human being. Do your own thing!

I can think of no more tragic image for the lonely dilemma of our shallow hedonistic attempts at "lovemaking" than the scene in *Last Tango in Paris* where an aging man and a young woman meet in a vacant apartment while each is hunting for a place to live, exchange glances, embrace, and have intercourse in one corner of the room, while he puts his hand over her mouth to keep her from speaking and mutters, "No names, no names!" Nameless, joyless, anonymous sex—the end result of our self-centered hedonism.

Spokesmen for the new hedonism as it has become institutionalized in the various manifestations of the so-called revolt against marriage would like us to think that they are offering us something new and important. They are not. What they offer are the inhumane values—disposability, irresponsibility, expendability, instant gratification—that make up the darkest side of the "system" itself.

While the trends in sexual behavior as mirrored in *Playboy* are blatantly hedonistic and self-centered, there are other challenges to marriage which are perhaps more respectable but just as threatening. The new attitudes toward marriage reflect new situations that have arisen in our transient modern society. One fourth of us move every year. The average length of time on one job is 4.3 years. We are people on the go who are infatuated with newness and change and who do not feel bound to our past. Many of the old secular props for marriage—the small, close-knit community, the extended family and stable home life—are no longer there. We become more interested in our own personal growth and well-being. People look for individuality (long an American frontier ideal) and equality (a twentieth-century infatuation). But how does one attain "freedom" and "emancipation" and remain in a traditional marriage? Many have answered that question with, "You cannot," and have proposed various "alternatives to traditional marriage."

For the millions of people who will divorce this year and will remarry in the future, the alternative to traditional monogamy will be serial monogamy. Youth have a point when they wonder why a series of divorces and remarriages is different from just "living with" a variety of partners. Why go through all of the expense and legal hassle of a formal marriage? Why not just live together until someone else better comes along?

The next step from serial monogamy is the proposal for a "contract" or "renewable" marriage in which both partners agree to live with each other for a stated length of time. Through a lawyer, they work out a contract for the ownership of their property and for the disposition of assets which are accumulated during their term of union. When the contract nears its expiry, both spouses assess the relationship and decide whether they wish to renew the contract for another term of marriage or part company. In his attack on conventional marriage, *Is Marriage Necessary?*,[1] Lawrence Casler agrees with Samuel Hopkins Adams's assessment of marriage as a "mutual suicide pact" and advocates a period of separation after the second year of married life for each spouse "to reconstitute his or her individuality."

Raymond Lawrence, while not taking the contract or the second-year separation approaches, argues for a more "flexible monogamy" in which one has a "*primary* genital sexual relationship" with a husband or wife but still keeps oneself free to "search for and explore other relationships, even to the point of genital sexual intimacy." Lawrence believes this arrangement will enable people to be secure in a primary sexual union without sacrificing the "stimulation of the new" that comes from pursuing other relationships.[2]

Monogamous unions are too restrictive, and emotionally and

sexually confining. That is the premise of Robert Thamm's *Beyond Marriage and the Nuclear Family.*[3] Segmented sex roles which lead to the subjection of women, the oppression of the elderly, and the emotional and intellectual deprivation of children are blamed on monogamy within the nuclear family. The venerable Carl Rogers, patron saint of encounter groupies and humanistic psychologists, agrees that monogamy is the cause rather than the cure of contemporary emotional disease. In *Becoming Partners,* Rogers praises today's liberated youth who eschew traditional modes of morality and, through their experimental living arrangements, "set the stage for a partnership revolution, a relationship revolution." In order to reach our full relational potential, Rogers urges us to drop such archaic and value-laden terms as "living in sin," "committing adultery," "fornication," and "homosexuality."[4] I fear that Dr. Rogers has clouded some very real and very important value questions with his own vague, pop-psychological jargon.

The specific proposed alternative which has attracted by far the most public attention is Nena and George O'Neill's *Open Marriage.* In the *Open Marriage,* both spouses perform as equal partners, free to explore various options which lead to selfhood.[5] Smothering togetherness, rigid roles, denial of self, and enforced fidelity—called characteristics of a "closed marriage"—are replaced by flexible roles, open and honest communication, privacy, growth, and freedom.

The emancipated couple in the *Open Marriage,* free from the imposed bondage of the "unrealistic expectations, unreasonable ideals, and mythological beliefs of a closed marriage,"[6] may engage in outside relationships including outside sexual relationships if they have "trust and mature love." "We are not recommending outside sex," say the O'Neills, "but we are not saying it should be avoided either."[7] Actually, sex is not mentioned that often by the O'Neills (which may be their avoidance of a major flaw in the *Open Marriage* proposal). The publisher's dust jacket says *Open Marriage* "is not just another manual of advice telling you how to make your marriage conform to somebody else's ideal." But the characteristics of the open marriage—individual autonomy, personal growth, affirmation of identity, honesty and truth, freedom to enjoy the friendship and intimate companionship of others, unconditional mutual trust, equal stature—sound rather idealistic. "Open" thus becomes a vague new cliché for a number of old ideals.

The book is naive in its view of human nature and imperialistic in its claims of which values (honesty, openness, equality) should outweigh other values (exclusiveness, fidelity, mutuality). The O'Neills have taken their ideal and prescribed it as a model for the rest of us. Personally, I have met few average males and females who can live with the knowledge that the other mate is engaging in sex with another, even if there is no deceit involved.

The *Open Marriage* appears to be addressed to white middle-class America which has become obsessed with its own desire for personal freedom at all costs and which has the requisite leisure and financial security to experiment with new relationships and modes of sexuality. *John and Mimi*[8] is a rather trivial account of a "sexually free marriage" in which each spouse receives encouragement from the other to experiment sexually with other people (which happens on every other page in the book, alone, in groups, bisexually, homosexually, and with a dizzying array of variations). I mention *John and Mimi* as an example of the open marriage taken to its worst excesses and as an example of a young couple who have traded puritanical obsession with the negatives of sex for an equally obsessive pursuit of its kinky joys. It is a strange kind of "freedom" we have obtained—a freedom which is always enslaved to its own relentless quest for something new to do with itself.

The "openness" of *John and Mimi* could occur only in a closed, like-minded counter-culture, free from worry about basic material needs or dependents (John and Mimi have no children and made no mention of siblings, parents, or community responsibilities). Have couples like John and Mimi achieved true sexual union or are they simply practicing a kind of sexual pathology? Research done by a number of social scientists indicates the possibility that sexually open marriages may be functional in today's pluralistic society.[9] Perhaps sexual exclusiveness is not a prerequisite for every vital marriage. But what works for a few cannot be absolutized for all. Are we ready to trust the future of our culture to these new experiments in marriage?

Running throughout many of the proposed alternatives to marriage is a curious kind of nativeté about basic human nature. For instance, most of the marriage alternatives, whether they advocate "open marriage" or simply "living together" tend to write off jealousy as something that partners must "rise above." This ignores the psychological data on the involuntary nature of our sentimental object attachments and their profound effect on our personalities. To argue that we ought to be "open" and "free" from such jealousy is to be not only naive but also unrealistic in an attempt to impose a selected set of ideological ideals upon a given fact of human nature (which is less than true "openness").

Even Carl Rogers, who is sympathetic to sexual and marital experimentation, after observing relationships with a number of "open" communes, is forced to admit that "jealousy is often an underestimated problem. . . . Indeed, I wonder whether jealousy is something simply conditioned by the culture or actually has a basic biological foundation, like territoriality?" [10] Yes, Dr. Rogers, perhaps it is "basic" for a human being to want one special human being who is most deeply intimate with him or her and no one else. Likewise, the so-called alternatives to marriage underestimate the basic need of each person for a reasonably secure, continuing, one-to-one relationship. Perhaps our monogamous marriage customs are built, not simply on societal convention, but on the basic psychological, biological, and spiritual needs of human beings. Or, to state it the way the church used to say it, marriage is based on the very nature and order of God's creation itself.

In summary, we must sound a loud *caveat emptor* in face of the new redefinitions of marriage, fidelity, adultery, etc. These new formulations work largely from the standpoint of idealistic, individualistic, hedonistic consumerism. What works for some may not work for the society as a whole. The current alternatives to marriage tend to be elitist and lack sufficient psychological and sociological data to qualify them as true alternatives. They generally ignore the problems related to a consequence of the majority of marriages—children. Marriage continues to be the mainstay of the socialization process in which norms are transmitted from one generation to the next. [11] To tamper thoughtlessly with such a basic institution is to invite future cultural breakdown, to say nothing of the individual human wreckage among those for whom these "experiments" prove unsuccessful.

To the old and new pagans who express their self-centered hedonism through assorted arrangements which attempt to allow individuals to "do their own thing" and still maintain the pretense of a truly intimate relationship, the Christian faith must affirm its own basic truth that life is better when it is lived in mutuality and self-giving rather than autonomy and self-seeking. To the cruder hedonists who would turn people into expendable playmates and to the more refined hedonists who cover their emotional isolationism under the cloak of such vagaries as "openness" and "freedom," we in the faith must maintain with the Bible that the goal of sexuality is *union*. As Karl Barth reminded us, "Coitus without co-existence is demonic."[12] It is a theological nonsequitur to speak of our sex as "intercourse" unless it is the true, total, self-giving, long-term *union* of every aspect of two people's lives.

There is much wrong with marriage today. Yet alternatives such as serial monogamy, short-term contracts, group marriage, swinging, open marriage, etc., suffer from all of the human problems which plague traditional marriage with the additional problems of the temporary and untested nature of these alternatives. Ultimately, marriage is probably here to stay. Dr. Sy Silverberg, a Toronto sexual therapist, after dealing with the actual human wreckage brought about by the "alternatives," makes this conclusion:

> Man must have long-term intimate relationships. . . . He must believe that there is someone who will accept and continue to care. You can't accomplish that with someone who has a casual or temporary commitment. As long as man craves for permanence in his life he will seek marriage.[13]

It is tragic in this age of loneliness and stifling, dehumanized technocracy, that many people have come to the erroneous conclusion that in order to grow, to mature, and to discover one's full potential, marriage must be avoided or radically changed. By that conclusion, these people may find that they have cut themselves off from the very means by which these human goals are achieved: a lifelong, caring, unifying, committed, growing relationship with another human being.

Notes for Chapter 3

[1] Lawrence Casler, *Is Marriage Necessary?* (New York: Human Sciences Press, 1974), p. 125.

[2] Raymond Lawrence, "Toward a More Flexible Monogamy," *Christianity and Crisis* (March 18, 1974), pp. 42-47.

[3] Robert Thamm, *Beyond Marriage and the Nuclear Family* (San Francisco: Canfield Press, 1975).

[4] Carl Rogers, *Becoming Partners: Marriage and Its Alternatives* (New York: Delacorte Press, 1972), pp. 213-214.

⁵Nena and George O'Neill, *Open Marriage: A New Lifestyle for Couples* (New York: Avon Books, 1972).

⁶*Ibid.*, p. 81.

⁷*Ibid.*, p. 254.

⁸John Lobell and Mimi Lobell, *John and Mimi: A Free Marriage* (New York: St. Martin's Press, 1972).

⁹See research cited by Robert T. Francoeur and Anna K. Francoeur in *Journal of Marriage and Family*, vol. 38, no. 1 (February, 1976), p. 195.

¹⁰Rogers, *op. cit.*, p. 158. Anna K. and Robert T. Francoeur in *Hot and Cool Sex: Cultures in Conflict* (New York: Harcourt Brace Jovanovich, Inc., 1974), p. 107, attribute jealousy and its desire for sexual exclusiveness to the rise of capitalism and private ownership of property!

¹¹William H. Jarrett, "Sociology and the Religious Prophets: Is the New Wine Any Better?" *Sociological Analysis* (Winter, 1974), pp. 233-239.

¹²Karl Barth, *Church Dogmatics, The Doctrine of Creation,* ed. G. W. Bromiley and T. F. Torrance (Edinburgh: T. & T. Clark, 1961), vol. 3, part 4, p. 133.

¹³Quoted by Paul Nowack in "Till Divorce Do Us Part," *Maclean's* (April 19, 1976), p. 31.

"A Wedding Sermon from a Prison Cell"

(May, 1943)

It is right and proper for a bride and bridegroom to welcome and celebrate their wedding day with a unique sense of triumph.... With the "Yes" that they have said to each other, they have by their free choice given a new direction to their lives; they have cheerfully and confidently defied all the uncertainties and hesitations with which, as they know, a lifelong partnership between two people is faced; and by their own free and responsible action they have conquered a new land to live in. Every wedding must be an occasion of joy that human beings can do such great things, that they have been given such immense freedom and power to take the helm in their life's journey. The children of the earth are rightly proud of being allowed to take a hand in shaping their own destinies, and something of this pride must contribute to the happiness of a bride and bridegroom. We ought not to be in too much of a hurry here to speak piously of God's will and guidance. It is obvious, and it should not be ignored, that it is your own very human wills that are at work here, celebrating their triumph; the course that you are taking at the outset is one that you have chosen for yourselves; what you have done and are doing is not, in the first place, something religious, but something quite secular. So you yourselves, and you alone, bear the responsibility for what no one can take from you; or, to put it more exactly, you... have all the responsibility for the success of your venture, with all the happiness that such responsibility involves.... Unless you can boldly say today: "That is *our* resolve, *our* love, *our* way," you are taking refuge in a false piety. "Iron and steel may pass away, but *our* love shall abide for ever."*

* Dietrich Bonhoeffer, *Letters and Papers from Prison, Revised Edition* (London: SCM Press, Ltd., © 1953, 1967). Reprinted with permission of Macmillan Publishing Co., Inc.

4

Old Puritans and New Perversions

Whenever things go too far in one direction, it will not be long before one can expect extremism in the other direction. Thus the excesses of the medieval state churches were sure to lead to the excesses of the Puritan iconoclasts. The radical disorder of the late sixties assured the Nixon-Agnew "law and order" backlash. Applying this historical principle to contemporary views on marriage, one cannot help wondering if the often irresponsible extremism of the revolt against marriage has precipitated the equally extreme reactionary defense of marriage. For every naive critic of marriage as the root of all our personal and social evils there is an equally naive defender of marriage as the magical formula that cures all ills. Both views are unrealistic. Marriage is an achievable challenge, but it is a difficult, demanding challenge.

While I am obviously a defender of the institution of marriage, I wish to disassociate my thoughts on marriage from some of marriage's other advocates. In this chapter we will examine one defense of marriage, that which is represented in books like *The Total Woman,* and ask ourselves if this view represents a strong defense of marriage or simply a sick perversion.

One of the most exciting and revolutionary events of our time is the resurgence of the Women's Movement around the world. The economic, psychological, and spiritual subjection of women have been continuing blots on the pages of human history. The oppression of women has taken its toll in the wasted talents, self-degradation, and subservience which women have suffered over the centuries. Marriage, as the basic institution for the nurturing of children and for relationships between males and females, has long been a focal point of criticism by feminists. Women rightly saw that there would be no equality or dignity for them in society as a whole as long as they suffered servitude and indignity in marriage.

Is it possible for a woman to achieve personal freedom and fulfillment within the context of Christian marriage? Many feminists say no, having decided that marriage is incompatible with women's liberation. In *The Church and the Second Sex*, Mary Daly says that marriage is little more than a socially approved system of "burial" and "imprisonment" for a woman which can only spell "disaster" for her true personhood.[1] While some radical feminists urge a kind of lesbian hedonism upon their sisters, Ms. Daly seems to advocate a new asceticism as an antidote to male attempts to make sex objects out of women. Forced to flatter or cajole the inflated male ego, to spend one's days in an endless round of petty household chores, to give up career aspirations in exchange for a full-time job as babysitter and domestic servant, many women, with help from the Pill, legal abortion, equal rights laws, and new openings in the job market, are forsaking marriage for what they see as newer and more fulfilling lifestyles.

While some of the more radical feminists' complaints against traditional marriage are legitimate, some of their charges and some of their proposals (i.e., lesbianism and asceticism) smack of the same kind of sexual isolationism and egoism that infect the new hedonists and many of the old sexist male chauvinists whom they abhor. The Christian faith maintains that true personal freedom and fulfillment come only in *union*, never in self-centered separation—be it the self-centeredness of a radical, male-hating feminist or the self-centeredness of a porcine, female-dominating, inflated, masculine lout.

But what kind of union? That is the central question for marriage. A union of equals where each person is free to go his or her own way? A union that lasts until someone else better comes along? A union where one is master and one is the obedient slave? Partly in response to the more extreme attacks upon marriage, partly out of fearful reaction to the changes that are taking place in our modern world, partly out of some continuing misunderstandings about sex and marriage within a Christian context, a phenomenon has recently swept America that deserves our attention—The Total Woman.

We live in curious times. It seems that we are forever falling into one extreme or another. We are a curious mix of puritan and sensualist, revolutionary and reactionary. Our curious polarities could not be better illustrated than by looking at the phenomenal success of Marabel Morgan's *The Total Woman.*[2] The reception of Kate Millet's *Sexual Politics,*[3] which sounded the clarion call for radical women's liberation, and Xaviera Hollander's *Happy Hooker,*[4] which extolled the joys of every possible expression of unrestrained feminine eroticism, pale into insignificance when compared to the success of the book by their ideologically opposite sister from Miami—Marabel Morgan. *The Total Woman* has sold well over one million copies and its sequel, *Total Joy,*[5] seems destined to surpass its forerunner in sales.

In *The Total Woman*, the happy Miami housewife gives her testimony of how she miraculously turned her blah and humdrum marriage to husband Charlie into a "perfect wave of libido" and "fireworks at breakfast" through adhering to an assortment of biblical precepts, Dale Carnegie platitudes, sexy outfits, and joyful submission to Charlie's wishes and whims. In the face of calls for wives to liberate themselves from subservience to their husbands, Mrs. Morgan would echo Shakespeare's sentiments in *The Taming of the Shrew,*

> Such duty as the subject owes the prince,
> Even such a woman oweth to her husband.
> —V, ii, 1.156

For the Total Woman, total joy comes only after she has submitted herself totally to her husband.

Mrs. Morgan's book is chock-full of advice for wives ("gals" as she calls them) on how to be suitably subservient to their dominant mates. "A Total Woman caters to her man's special quirks, whether it be in salads, sex, or sports."[6] "When your husband asks you to do something, he expects it to be done without reminding you. The next time he delegates a job to you, write it down."[7] Mrs. Morgan bases her call to female submission on, of all people, the apostle Paul. Ephesians 5:22 is the verse which is used as the Total Woman's guiding principle:

The biblical remedy for marital conflict is stated, "You wives must submit to your husbands' leadership in the same way you submit to the Lord." God planned for woman to be under her husband's rule.[8]

From Paul's words on submission, Mrs. Morgan derives the following analogy:

> ... the husband is king, and his wife is queen. In a royal marriage, the king's decision is the final word, for his country and the queen alike. The queen is certainly not his slave, for she knows where her powers lie. She is queen. She, too, sits on a throne. She has the right, and in fact, the responsibility to express her feelings, but of course, she does so in a regal way. . . . if there is a difference of opinion, it is the king who makes the final decision. . . .
>
> What if the king makes the wrong decision? . . . The queen is still to follow him, forthwith. A queen shall not nag or buck her king's decision after it is decreed. Remember those speedy trials, gals![9]

These are strong words for modern wives, especially since they are based on the injunctions of one no less than Paul himself. But is this really what Paul meant by "Wives, be subject to your husbands. . . ."?

Let us look at the entire text of Paul's household code in Ephesians 5. While Mrs. Morgan fails to quote it in its entirety, it should be noted that the section opens with the words, in verse 21, "Be subject *to one another* (italics mine), out of reverence for Christ." Subjection does seem to be the primary principle for marital relationships here:

> Wives, be subject to your husbands, as to the Lord. For the husband is the head of the wife as Christ is the head of the church, his body, and is himself its Savior. As the church is subject to Christ, so let wives also be subject in everything to their husbands. Husbands, love your wives, as Christ loved the church and gave himself up for her, that he might sanctify her, having cleansed her by the washing of water with the word. . . . Even so husbands should love their wives as their own bodies. He who loves his wife loves himself. For no man ever hates his own flesh, but nourishes and cherishes it, as Christ does the church, because we are members of his body. "For this reason a man shall leave his father and mother and be joined to his wife, and the two shall become one flesh." This mystery is a profound one, and I am saying that it refers to Christ and the church (Ephesians 5:22-32).

Biblical scholars feel that Paul borrowed this code and its listing of conjugal duties from Hellenistic Judaism.[10] Paul simply borrowed conventional wisdom of the day to which he applied a Christian veneer ("in the Lord"). Here is a typical elaboration of feminine subservience in marriage.

Or is it? A closer look at this passage reveals that Paul has converted this traditional Near Eastern folk wisdom into a true Christian theology of marriage. But it is an easily misunderstood theology unless we read it with care. Verse 21 (which Mrs. Morgan conveniently omits) sets the pattern. Subjection is the primary principle here, but it is *mutual* subjection based, not upon vows, or compatibility, or even love, but upon the relationship of the husband and wife to Christ. The nature of Christian marriage is thus derived, not from an empirical study of marriage as a social institution, not from the various characteristics of males and females, but from our relationship with Christ who reveals to us the true intended nature of our relationships with one another. For Paul, the human relationship of marriage derives its form and its standards from the divine-human relationship of Christ and his church.

The passage first deals with the duties of a wife within this pattern of mutual submission. Paul compares her submission to the submission of the church to Christ. But this could not mean, as Mrs. Morgan assumes, that wives are to worship, to obey unquestioningly, or to treat their husbands like gods. That would make the wife an idolatress, offering to a man what she should only offer to God, and would make the husband a blasphemer, assuming godlike dominance over another person. The wife's love for her husband could only be seen as love for Christ in the sense that Jesus said, ". . . as you did it to one of the least of these my brethren, you did it to me" (Matthew 25:40).[11] Admittedly, "submission" or "subjection" of any kind is an unpopular attitude in today's independence-infatuated culture. But, from a Christian point of view, there can be no surer path to personal fulfillment than the submission of oneself to another person. As John Calvin once said:

> God has bound us so strongly to each other that no man [person] ought to endeavor to avoid subjection; and where love reigns, mutual services will be rendered. . . . But as nothing is more irksome to the mind of man than this mutual subjection, he directs us to *the fear of Christ*.

"Mutual submission" is also enjoined in 1 Peter 5:5; Romans 12:10; and Philippians 2:3. Calvin sees this submission as a graceful, voluntary humbling of our selfish pride so "that we may not be ashamed of serving our neighbors" even as Christ has served us.[12]

The rest of the passage deals with the duties of husbands toward their wives. Paul seems to feel that husbands need more guidance in fulfilling their duties than wives! One expects a Near Eastern writer of the day to stress the subservience of the wife. That is typical. One does not expect such a radical (for that day) and unqualified demand for the submission of the husband. Paul says that husbands must love their wives even as Christ has loved the church. Any "lordship" which the husband may have is like the lordship of Christ—the Suffering Servant who suffers, submits, and gives everything in order that his beloved (the church) might be exalted. Any claim for male monarchial domination which attempts to base itself on this passage does injustice to the peculiar nature of Jesus' lordship as depicted in the gospel. What kind of lord and master lays down his life for another person? Only the lord who sees his lordship based upon sacrificial love and humble service. That is the Christlike "lordship" that is demanded of husbands. Here is a radical new image for male-female relationships in marriage. The marriage bond is transformed from one in which the wife is simply subjected to the husband without qualification into one in which the husband is to devote himself unreservedly in love for his wife. The old household code is turned upside down, and the emphasis is shifted from the duty of the wife to her husband, to the husband's love for his wife. Perhaps "devotion" is a more accurate translation of Paul's thought than "submission."

Paul's theology of marriage as mutual submission in Christ is concluded with a quote from Genesis 2:24 on the unity of a husband and wife. As stated in our last chapter, this theme of unity figured prominently in Jesus' own statements about sex and marriage: ". . . the two shall become one." Therefore, when a husband loves his wife, he is loving his own flesh, his own true self. There is no question here of equality between two separate but equals, certainly no question of a union between a dominant person and a subservient person. The image here is of a union that is so intimate, so inextricably bound, that "to love the other is to love one's self," as the Great Commandment puts it. It is a union no less miraculous and mysterious than the union of Christ with the church in which, in Paul's view, the church becomes the very body of Christ. A similar union is effected when a man and a woman unite in mutual submission "in the Lord." The stress in the entire passage is a stress upon *union* rather than mere duty, union achieved by loving devotion to one another.

Mrs. Morgan tries to convince us that the subservience which she advocates is not enslavement. She claims that the Total Woman is not a slave because she chooses, by her own free will, to adapt to her husband's way.[13] But slavery, whether voluntary or involuntary, is still servitude—degrading, dehumanizing, and an affront to the maturity and freedom which Christ has bestowed upon us. The mutual submission and union of Christian marriage leave absolutely no room for servitude on the part of either member of the marriage. They call upon a couple to commit themselves to each other, totally, permanently, unreservedly—precisely the same way in which Jesus

Christ has completely committed himself to us.

The Total Woman technique demeans not only the woman, but also the man. Behind Mrs. Morgan's call for female submission is a not-so-subtle attempt to manipulate the husband through the pretense of "revering and worshiping" him. If a wife flatters her man, praises his puny muscles, meets him at the door each evening in transparent, pink (*hot* pink is prescribed) sleepwear, and fulfills his every desire, *then* "he in turn will gratefully respond by trying to make it up to her and grant her desires. He may even want to spoil her with goodies."[14] Sex, love, and submission thus become feminine ploys which the sly wife uses to entice her unwary husband into fulfilling her desires. Is this the kind of self-giving, unifying love of which Paul speaks? How is it possible for a husband to feel true intimacy and lifelong growth when he is living with a cunning consort, an underling rather than a marital companion?

There are some values in Marabel Morgan's Total Woman technique for a happy marriage. For one thing, the Total Woman has a healthy, if sometimes tasteless, appreciation for the joys of sex in marriage. Mrs. Morgan has redeemed marital sex from the stuffy admonitions that have clouded most fundamentalist Christian discussions of marriage. As far as the Total Woman is concerned, ". . . sex is for the marriage relationship only, but within those bounds. . . . Sex is as clean and pure as eating cottage cheese."[15] In what has been labeled as a "Kama Sutra for Christians," Mrs. Morgan advocates new nighties, Saran Wrap, pink baby-doll pajamas, and white boots after bubble baths in order to put zing back in drab sex.[16] While some of her suggestions come perilously close to the kind of kinky sex techniques of *The Joy of Sex*, no one can accuse Mrs. Morgan of puritanical prudishness in the name of piety.

Many women, trapped in dull, lifeless marriages, have undoubtedly found hope and encouragement through *The Total Woman*. The phenomenal success of Mrs. Morgan's books attest to the deep need among many people, particularly women, for a new vision of how a man and a woman can live together without destroying themselves in a slow death of emotional, sexual, and spiritual estrangement masquerading as marriage. But there is tragedy lying behind the cheerful pages of *The Total Woman's* helpful hints for marital happiness. It is the tragedy of loneliness in the midst of togetherness, subservience legitimized as love, manipulation of another person under the guise of sex. Rather than giving women lasting hope for the future, *The Total Woman* attests to our present helplessness. It legitimizes and gives theological justification to some of the worst aspects of contemporary marriage in its most perverted forms. It encourages a man and woman to retain their individuality, their separate and unequal roles and expectations, and to bargain with one another for their respective bits of marital bliss.

Union—the true goal of marriage—cannot be achieved between a master and a slave no matter how devoted the slave or how benevolent the master. It cannot be won through manipulation, sexual bargaining, or one-sided submission. No, true union comes only in mutual self-giving. We give out of our own dignity in Christ, realizing that in totally giving oneself to another, one receives one's true selfhood in return. It is a union which fulfills and completes us because it is the union which enables us to be what we as men and women were created to be. Marriage does require total response and commitment, but not from the woman alone. Marriage is a meeting which takes place in the most intimate depths of our being, calling for total, lifelong, loving commitment to one another; no less than the kind of commitment which Christ has shown toward us.

Notes for Chapter 4

[1] Mary Daly, *The Church and the Second Sex* (New York: Harper & Row, Publishers, Inc., 1975), pp. 29-35.

[2] Marabel Morgan, *The Total Woman* (Old Tappan, N.J.: Fleming H. Revell Company, 1973).

[3] Kate Millet, *Sexual Politics* (New York: Doubleday & Company, Inc., 1970).

[4] Xaviera Hollander, *The Happy Hooker* (New York: Dell Publishing Co., Inc., 1972).

[5] Marabel Morgan, *Total Joy* (Old Tappan, N.J.: Fleming H. Revell Company, 1976).

[6] Morgan, *The Total Woman*, p. 55.

[7] *Ibid.*, p. 32.

[8] *Ibid.*, p. 69. The biblical quote is from *The Living Bible.*

[9] *Ibid.*, p. 71.

[10] Reginald H. Fuller, "Sunday Scripture Readings," *Worship* (June-July, 1973), pp. 356-357.

[11] Elizabeth Achtemeier, *The Committed Marriage* (Philadelphia: The Westminster Press, 1976), p. 85.

[12] "Mutual Submission," *Christianity Today* (November 22, 1974), p. 42.

[13] Morgan, *The Total Woman*, pp. 69-71.

[14] *Ibid.*, p. 71.

[15] *Ibid.*, p. 111.

[16] "The New Housewife Blues," *Time* (March 14, 1977), pp. 62-70.

Dearly beloved friends, we are gathered together here in the sight of God, and in the face of his congregation, to join together this man and this woman in holy matrimony, which is an honorable estate, instituted of God in paradise in the time of man's innocency, signifying unto us the mystical union, that is betwixt Christ and his Church: which holy estate Christ adorned and beautified with his presence and first miracle that he wrought in Cana of Galilee, and is commended of Saint Paul to be honorable among all men, and therefore is not to be enterprised nor taken in hand unadvisedly, lightly, or wantonly, to satisfy men's carnal lusts and appetites, like brute beasts that have no understanding, but reverently, discreetly, advisedly, soberly, and in the fear of God, duly considering the causes for which matrimony was ordained. One was, the procreation of children to be brought up in the fear and nurture of the Lord, and praise of God. Secondly, it was ordained for a remedy against sin, and to avoid fornication, that such persons as have not the gift of continency might marry, and keep themselves undefiled members of Christ's body. Thirdly, for the mutual society, help, and comfort, that the one ought to have of the other, both in prosperity and adversity: into the which holy estate these two persons present come now to be joined. Therefore, if any man can show any just cause why they may not lawfully be joined together, let him now speak, or else hereafter forever hold his peace.*

*"The Form of Solemnization of Matrimony"
The Book of Common Prayer, 1559

5

The Risk of Union

The groom and groomsmen wore snow white, long-tail tuxedos. The groom wore an ice blue oversized camellia. The groomsmen's boutonnieres were white carnations.

The reception and dinner were held on the back lawn. Barbeque was served along with the three-tiered blue wedding cake over a blue fountain and a chocolate, guitar-shaped groom's cake. The pink champagne fountain featured a cluster of 50 blue and white helium balloons attached to its top.

The reception began with a dance by the bride and groom to "The Blue Danube Waltz." When the cake was cut, 1000 helium balloons were released, all blue and white and imprinted with the names of the couple and wedding date.

The reception music featured The Morris Sisters and The Morgan Country Grass.[1]

"The Service of Holy Matrimony" was a latecomer to Christian worship services. In its present form it represents a curious amalgam of pagan customs and Christian beliefs, theological statements and legal requirements. Also, the above newspaper account of a marriage reminds us that many marriages are often a blend of the sublime and the ridiculous! Such is the nature of matrimony.

In pagan culture, marriage was simply a legal act, a contract between two persons involving stipulations about property rights, inheritance, dowry, etc. Expressions like "to have and to hold" and "'till death us do part" are lawyer's talk which the church adapted for its own ritual of marriage. Likewise, the giving of the woman, vows, linking of hands, and witnesses are holdovers from earlier civic acts. Many stated and unstated rituals of marriage continue ancient pagan

57

customs. For instance, the bride feeding the groom the wedding cake relates to the Roman custom of the bride baking a wedding cake on the groom's hearth and then feeding the groom the cake to symbolize her acceptance of the groom's household gods.

It seems as if the church has been hesitant to claim the solemnization of matrimony with all of marriage's pagan and legal accretions. At first the church simply added its blessing following the secular contract of marriage. In the Middle Ages, marriages got as far as the front porch of the church. They were performed there by the clergy since the clergy were usually the only people in town who could read or write. By the sixteenth century, marriage finally entered the church where it has remained as an alternative to civil ceremonies. Witnessing the ostentation, extravagance, and absence of any real commitment to the Christian faith in many contemporary weddings, some people in the church wonder if we should have let marriage in the door in the first place!

Personally, I am not yet willing for the church to withdraw from its role in the sealing of marriage vows. It is my contention that this is too important a life event and that the church has too great an investment in the union of men and women and the nature of family life to acquiesce and let a couple "do their own thing" or let the state alone determine the nature of marriage. Within the event of marriage there are pastoral, evangelical, and educational opportunities for affirming what our faith proclaims about the equality of men and women, the meaning of sexuality, the nature of the family, the challenge of love, and the necessity for commitment. Just because the Christian community has often corrupted marriage by capitulation to the wishes and whims of brides, florists, and musicians, this is no reason to relinquish our duty to guide people at this significant occasion. A new boldness in the place of our accustomed timidity would do much to retrieve our rituals for marriage from their insipid state. In the remaining chapters of this book, I will attempt to develop a theology of Christian marriage, referring frequently to the old "Service of Holy Matrimony" from the 1559 *Book of Common Prayer* since this service relates to the most ancient Christian marriage practices and beliefs and is the model for contemporary marriage services in nearly every Protestant denomination. Having spoken of the Christian attitude toward sexuality, having heard some contemporary attacks upon marriage, let us now turn to the task of formulating a contemporary Christian theology of marriage.

Before examining the marriage service from a theological point of view, let us begin by looking at the rituals of marriage from the standpoint of anthropology. An anthropologist would tell us that the very existence of the elaborate rituals of marriage, absurd though they may often seem, attests to the deep human significance of this event. While many of our contemporary marriage customs owe more to pagan practices than to Christian creeds, all these carefully prescribed and patterned acts, whether they be the words spoken by the minister, the seating of the bride's mother, the playing of music from Wagner, or the agonizing over the selection of a new china pattern, have developed as the means of helping a couple unite in marriage. Anthropologically speaking, the marriage ritual is a "rite of passage" in which a man and woman separate from their single status, pass through a series of traditional, ritualized words and acts, and enter into a new union with one another.[2]

As a "rite of passage," moving us from one state of existence to another, ritual helps us to cope with the anxiety and pain that is occasioned by life's transitions. That is why such potentially difficult times as death, graduation, the inauguration of our nation's president, and marriage are surrounded by a rigidly patterned series of stated and unstated ritual acts. Even couples with a nominal religious commitment will often feel a strong need for some public, ritualized recognition of their marriage and will seek out a minister and a church for the ceremony. Even in the secular Soviet Union, there is an elegant "Hall of Marriages" in Moscow where the state does its best to provide a marital rite of passage for Soviet couples. There is an inherent need for community support in crossing the threshold, a necessity for education into the nature of the new status, and a desire for public recognition of a couple's commitment. The rituals of marriage perform all these functions.

Finally, an anthropologist (or psychologist) would tell us that wherever there is rigidly prescribed, widely practiced, and elaborately performed ritual, then that ritual is evidence of the high level of anxiety and risk that is related to the event. There is a kind of rationality behind many of our seemingly irrational rituals. We need them in order to get by. Transition, the separation from one state of being and the incorporation into another, usually involves risk—the risk of leaving the comfortable predictability of our former state and journeying into some unknown, unpredictable territory of life. And yet the risk and its attendant anxiety are necessary if we are to grow and achieve our full God-given potential. But the risk is still painful. One part of us wants to stay; the other part wants to move forward. One part wants to let go; the other wants to hold on. There is risk in the act of marriage. The Service of Marriage, however and wherever it is performed, speaks to that risk and it is to this often overlooked element of risk in marriage that we now turn.

In the earlier part of this book we examined some of the contemporary alternatives to traditional marriage and noted the risky nature of these untested modes of living together. While delineating the risks in contemporary sexual and marital experimentation, it would be misleading if we did not admit to the risks in traditional monogamy. A monogamous, committed, permanent, satisfying relationship does not come easily. Putting any man and woman in such close physical, emotional, and spiritual proximity exposes them to all sorts of hazards. It is risky to dare to link your future with another person's, to accept all that person's strengths and weaknesses and ask that person to accept yours. And yet, it is precisely that kind of bold risk that the Christian faith asks of people. It asks us, in marriage, to venture out, to expose ourselves to the complex and unfathomable reality of another human being. It is that risk taking that makes marriage unpopular for many people today.

Tom Wolfe has called us "The Me Generation," with each person consumed by a passionate love for Number One, assuming that the world begins with his birth, ends with his death, and "can be endured only by constant focus on his own selfish ego, pondering and pandering to his Me." [3] In this self-centered, brave, new world where Jefferson's "pursuit of happiness" has run riot, "liberation" too often means liberation from responsibility for anyone but oneself. "Freedom" becomes "free to be me apart from you." "Maturity" degenerates into the adolescent fantasy of growing up "on my own," doing my "own thing" away from you. The "Me Generation" is depicted in Ingmar Bergman's film, *Scenes from a Marriage*. In the film, a married couple, Johan and Marianne, are followed through the sad dissolution of their marriage. Marianne has become "liberated" and now vaunts her newfound freedom which she has attained through what Johan bitterly satirizes as the "new women's gospel." She does appear happier, more self-secure, and in a better emotional state than Johan. But she appears curiously driven and trapped in her new "freedom." In scene five, Marianne screams out at Johan in drunken rage:

Do you suppose that I've gone through all I have, and come out on the other side and started a life of my own which every day I'm thankful for, just to take charge of you and see that you don't go to the dogs because you're so weak and full of self-pity? . . . I've hardened myself.[4]

This suggests that Marianne is not as free as she claims. She is only free to be herself if she defines herself apart from or opposed to another person. How can freedom be equated with egotism, irresponsibility, and isolation? How can true selfhood be equated with selfishness?

Somewhere Martin Luther speaks of sin as *cor incurratum in se*, "the heart all curled up inside itself." Christianity has traditionally said that the most demonic servitude of all is enslavement to oneself. There is no freedom in escape from our responsibility to others; for in responding to another, in letting another person make claims upon me, and in laying claim to that person to fulfill some of my needs, I discover my true self. Curling up inside myself, seeking personal growth by turning within myself, and withdrawing into excessive concern for my own needs lead only to the frustration of wandering in the circular maze of the narrow boundaries of my own limited ego. The longest journey we ever travel is the difficult trip from the "I" to the "You." But without undertaking that risky pilgrimage, we will remain stunted and forever unfulfilled. The "Me Generation" seeks union without risk and love without self-giving. This is impossible.

Of course, all this has been said before, and much more pointedly than I have said it, in the book of Genesis. The first chapters of Genesis speak of the created union of a man and woman, the sin of separation, and the divine call to unite "as one flesh." The earliest of the two creation stories, Genesis 1:1–2:4*a*, states that both male and female are created in the image of God. Contrary to Paul's views in 1 Corinthians 11:7, no differentiation is made here in the way that men and women possess that image. In the second creation story, Genesis 2:4*b*-24, man is shaped from the dust of the ground, woman from the rib of man. This in no way implies superior or inferior status for the man or woman. "Adam" in the story is the Hebrew word for "humanity." The man is alone. This loneliness is seen by the Creator as wrong; so a companion is needed and woman is created. The story says that originally the man and woman were "one flesh" and, after the creation of woman, they desire to restore their oneness. This, for Genesis 2, becomes the basis of marriage, "Therefore a man leaves his father and his mother and cleaves to his wife and they become one flesh" (Genesis 2:24). Sex is thus an act of re-union. Contrary to being a subservient afterthought, the woman is simply the often neglected half of the male's incomplete image of God.

From the beginning the Bible affirms that marriage is no mere social convention or cultural idiosyncrasy. It is part of the Creator's original intention. As Jesus said, ". . . from the beginning of creation, 'God made them male and female'" (Mark 10:6). The old Roman Catholic natural law arguments for marriage have much to commend them. Any fool can look at a woman and see certain natural endowments for motherhood. A cursory comparative glance at the respective male and female anatomies can see evidence of a certain biological congruence between the man and the woman. Reality is structured, the world is created, in such a way that marriage is a necessary part of it. It is the created mutuality, this inherent drive toward union, which is one of God's greatest gifts. We need one another in order to complete our broken images of our God.

Throughout the Bible, the union of a man and woman in marriage is analogously applied to the divine will for union with humanity. Israel is frequently spoken of as God's wife (Isaiah 50:1; 54:4-6; Jeremiah 3:20) or bride (Isaiah 62:5; Jeremiah 2:2; Hosea 2:16-20). In the New Testament, Jesus is compared to a bridegroom (Mark 2:19-20; John 3:29; Matthew 25:1-13). We have already noted the Pauline use of the union of husband and wife as a symbol of Christ's union with the church. In Revelation, the advent of the kingdom of God is depicted as a marriage (Revelation 19:6-9; 21:9-11). Sexual intercourse and the emotional, legal, and spiritual union of a man and woman in marriage are made more meaningful by comparing them to the total self-giving of Christ to his people. "It is not good that man should be alone . . ." (Genesis 2:18). In place of our isolation and loneliness, God has given us the possibility of union and relationship.

In an age of self-conscious independency and suffocating inwardness, where a myriad of techniques and therapies promise salvation through "discovery of my self," "doing your own thing," "survival of the fittest," the mutuality, union, and relationship of Christian marriage has become a revolutionary endeavor. "Revolution" means conversion or change, and conversion always implies risk. The bold ones in our modern world are not those who carefully guard their own autonomy and jealously protect their own exaggerated individuality. Such timid self-centeredness has been the conventional behavior of sinful humanity since time began. No, the bold ones in our age are the ones who dare to risk themselves by giving themselves to another person in order to grow into some new and more completed selves.

Contrary to popular belief, marriage does not call for subjection to another person or suppression of one's personality. It calls for true freedom. Our "liberation" comes not from some heroic exercise of one's own ego. It comes from a new vision of who I am created to be, of being free to be all that I can be for myself *and* another person. As Elizabeth Achtemeier noted in her fine book on marriage, the human being conceived of as an isolated center of independent will is the very antithesis of true humanity.[5] To paraphrase Augustine, "We were made for Communion, and our hearts are restless until they find unity with thee."

The Christian marriage ceremony illustrates the belief that a deep sexual and emotional encounter between two people requires a revolution in which both turn away from their self-centeredness. To unite with another person, one must risk oneself in a rite of passage which entails the death of the old self and the resurrection of the new. Within the ceremony itself there are numerous images of this death and resurrection, such as "for this reason a man leaves his father and mother" and "the two become one flesh." To remain your same old self with your same old individualistic point of view is not enough. Many marriages fail because the partners fail to comprehend the radical transformation which is demanded of them in marriage. Conversely, many divorces fail because the divorcees fail to comprehend how their marriage, unsatisfactory though it may have been, transformed two individuals into a new union, a bond which can never be finally broken. The risk of union is the risk that your old, separated, former self will never be the same!

Jesus' objections to divorce were related to this view of the nature of the marriage bond. When Jesus quotes Genesis 2:24, "They shall be one flesh," he uses the word "flesh" in the frequent Old Testament sense of the entire being or personality of the human person.[6] To "become one flesh" with the marriage partner is to become united in a profound ontological transformation. Jesus therefore forbids divorce, unlike the Old Testament, because the union of marriage effects such a radical change in the man and woman that a recovery of their former selves is ontologically impossible. One can never fully dissolve the marriage union because once it is done and finished, it remains a part of who we are for as long as life endures. As Thomas

Aquinas said, even God "cannot make what is past not to have been."[7] Our identity is constituted by our history, including our sexual, emotional, and relational history. All the unions in which I have participated make me who I am. This is more true of marriage, the union of marriage being the most intimate, all-encompassing, and demanding of any human relationship. The risk of marriage is the creative risk of finding yourself being transformed into a new being while in the presence of that other with whom you have joined in love. Marriage is always meeting, welcoming that stranger into the innermost depths of your heart, and in turn being received by the one who begins as a stranger and ends as your most intimate companion.

The thundering primal word of Genesis, that a man should cleave to his wife and become one flesh with her, is both a command and a promise.[8] It is a command, calling us to press on to that unity which perfects our incomplete selves and helps us find our lives by losing them in one another. Both the command and the promise are this: the impossible—unity in a world of disunity and self-giving in a world of self-seeking—is possible. The two can become one and thus signify to the world "the mystical union that is betwixt Christ and his Church," as the marriage service says it. This union comes as a promised gift. For what God commands he also gives. In other words, marriage does require risk, but it is not a foolhardy risk or a blind leap with another person into an uncertain future. The risk of union is a reasonable risk and a leap of faith taken, not because of our great confidence in ourselves and our ability to love another person, but because of our knowledge of the created order of the world and our confidence in God and his unlimited ability to "make all things new"—even us.

Notes for Chapter 5

[1] The Tuscaloosa, Alabama, *News* (August 20, 1976).

[2] A. van Gennep, *The Rites of Passage* (Chicago: University of Chicago Press, 1961).

[3] Quoted in *The Charlotte Observer* (May 15, 1977) p. 3B.

[4] From *Scenes from a Marriage*, quoted by Janet Karsten Larson, "Schemes from a Marriage," *The Christian Century* (June 1, 1977), pp. 538-539.

[5] Elizabeth Achtemeier, *The Committed Marriage* (Philadelphia: The Westminster Press, 1976), pp. 94-97.

[6] Kenneth Grayston, "Flesh," *A Theological Word Book of the Bible,* ed. Alan Richardson (New York: Macmillan, Inc., 1950), p. 83.

[7] John Macquarrie, "The Nature of the Marriage Bond," *Theology* (May, 1975), p. 235.

[8] G. R. Dunstan, quoted by Helen Oppenheimer in "Is the Marriage Bond an Indissoluble 'Vinculum'?" *Theology* (May, 1975), p. 243.

When You Are Old

When you are old and grey and full of sleep,
And nodding by the fire, take down this book,
And slowly read, and dream of the soft look
Your eyes had once, and of their shadows deep;

How many loved your moments of glad grace,
And loved your beauty with love false or true;
But one man loved the pilgrim soul in you,
And loved the sorrows of your changing face.

And bending down beside the glowing bars,
Murmur, a little sadly, how love fled
And paced upon the mountains overhead
And hid his face amid a crowd of stars.*

*Reprinted with permission of Macmillan Publishing Co., Inc., from *Collected Poems* by William Butler Yeats. © 1906 by Macmillan Publishing Co., Inc., renewed 1934 by William Butler Yeats.

6

The Challenge of Commitment

In a 1974 issue of *Today's Ministry*, Roy DeLamotte offered a tongue-in-cheek proposal for a new kind of marriage service to suit contemporary mores—"The Situational Wedding:"[1]

> The Situational Ceremony is based on the fact that in today's world right and wrong are decided on the basis of the total human situation at any given moment.

This new wedding modifies existing rites in the interest of "freedom" and "authentic individuality." The minister begins the ceremony with the charge to the bride and groom:

> Dearly beloved, we are gathered here in the presence of the Existing Situation to join together this man and this woman in situational wedlock, which is a temporary estate, signifying unto us the fulfillment of our authentic individuality as currently interpreted. It is therefore not to be entered into nervously, reluctantly, or with any anxiety over permanent entrapment by the partner or by some alleged Divinity with ideas of His own.

> I warn you solemnly that if the vows you are about to take be kept steadfast in defiance of changing circumstances, for better for worse, for richer for poorer, in sickness and in health, you could very well end up driving last year's car or nursing someone who's lost her looks. Do ye solemnly promise not to take these vows in any such inhibitory sense but joyously, freely, and with minds and imaginations open to all that the future may bring?

After the bride and groom give the appropriate response, "Er-ah-maybe," the "vows" are administered in a carefully reworked form which has removed any hint of permanence or commitment on the part of the bride and groom:

> Few human ties are more fleeting, few vows less binding, than those you now assume. Tom, wilt thou have this woman to be thy lawfully wedded wife, to live together in the temporary state of matrimony? Wilt thou hug her, kiss her, and thoroughly enjoy her, and forsaking all others who are less attractive at the moment, keep thee only unto her so long as ye both shall find the arrangement satisfactory?

To which the groom responds, "I may."

DeLamotte's Situational Wedding provoked a storm of enraged reader response which verified not only the humorlessness of many clergy but also how close this service resembles many people's approach to marriage. Ours is an age that takes a dim view of permanent commitments.

As goes marriage, so goes the family. Pollster Daniel Yankelovich's massive study of current family attitudes, *The American Family Report: Raising Children in a Changing Society,*[2] found that nearly half of America's younger families stress freedom over authority, self-fulfillment over material success, and duty to self over duty to others—including their spouses and even their children. Yankelovich heard today's parents saying to their children, "We will not sacrifice for you, because we have our own lives to lead. But when you are grown, you owe us nothing." This includes their belief that unhappy parents should not remain married for the sake of the children.[3]

If there is one thing we fear more than risk (chapter 5), it is permanence. For Christian marriage to claim that sex, love, and personal growth are best only when experienced within the context of a lifelong, unconditional commitment is to challenge some of the basic assumptions of modern society. In his frightening book, *Future Shock,* Alvin Toffler has described contemporary America as the "throw-away society."[4] Rapidly changing fashions, continually shifting fads, and disposable gadgets and products with built-in obsolescence make us a nation of waste-makers in which, as we noted earlier, not only things but also people become disposable. Toffler even suggests disposable marriage partners, each one suited to our rapidly changing stages in life. After all, who can expect permanence in human relationships in our future-shocked world?

We have been called "neophiles," obsessive lovers of the new. We show a low tolerance for repetition, pattern, and sameness. "Love" becomes an ecstatic experience of orgasmic release occurring in an unrepeatable moment of bliss. In fact, ·repetition or duplication somehow seems to rob this so-called "love" of its significance for us. We seek out new sex positions and novel techniques of enticement in *The Joy of Sex* and *The Total Woman* in order to keep our love life fresh, new, and invigorating. Anthropologist Margaret Mead says that she has seen this fear of repetition and permanence in no other society.[5] Americans say, "What is old is bad," whereas the majority of humanity say, "What is old is good." In other cultures what is permanent and trustworthy is what is valuable. Perhaps our fear of permanence is due to our technology with its rapid-fire change, or our transient uprootedness (you know how often the average American moves or changes jobs), or the shallowness and youthfulness of our comparatively young culture. Whatever the causes, the fear of permanence and long-term commitment have become striking characteristics of our national life.

The new culture presents us with a curious blend of a loudly proclaimed new interest in "interpersonal relations" combined with the same old individualistic self-centeredness. On the one hand, there seems to be a new enthusiasm for social responsibilities: social activism, communal living, combined efforts to clean up the environment, coalitions for political change, etc. On the other hand, there is its continuing fascination with what could only be called a form of anarchy in its attempts to eliminate any form of long-term commitment from life. Behind many of the calls to free ourselves from the depersonalized controls of the old authoritarian culture and the stifling restraints of narrow parochialism is a romantic desire for freedom from all social conditions. This is simply to exchange one form of loneliness for another.[6] Anarchy is an exchange of the worst aspects of bureaucratic, materialistic culture for the equally destructive aspects of the new irresponsible, autonomous, transient culture. Our adolescent desire for discipleship without church affiliation, democracy without informed participation, community without commitment, society without structure, and sex without marriage presents a continuing source of frustration to our noblest attempts to "get it all together."

As our 1960s' belief in political answers withers, the cult of personal relations intensifies, issuing forth in our current wave of withdrawal symptoms in the 1970s. Witness the development in our time of the myriad techniques for autosalvation and narcissism

disguised as therapy ("est," "I'm O.K. You're O.K.," The Human
Potential Movement, and so on). The tragedy is that, by their stress
on noncommitment and continual change, they are self-defeating. As
some have noted, the new human potential techniques actually
frustrate human fulfillment since they advise people against great
involvement in love and friendship and against dependence on other
people, factors which themselves have contributed to crises in human
relationships. To define "growth" as a continual process of shedding
our old selves and relationships, taking on new interests, and
adapting with protean ease to each new moment on this basis of the
dictates of the moment is to deny the human need to grow to maturity
through continuity with one's old selves and the people of one's past.
Growth requires building upon our past and sticking with a
relationship until it matures rather than frantically leaping from one
person to the next or aimlessly drifting through a never-ending
succession of transitory human encounters which masquerade as
"relationships."

Against the transitory, uncommitted, rootless qualities of modern
life, Christian marriage sounds the call to commitment. There is a
kind of grimness in every marriage service—an honest, realistic
admission that life has its "worse" side. I am fond of that phrase in the
Book of Common Prayer, deleted by prudish Victorians, in which the
minister warns the couple that marriage is not to be taken

> . . . unadvisedly, lightly, or wantonly, to satisfy men's carnal lusts and
> appetites, like brute beasts that have no understanding, but reverently,
> discreetly, advisedly, soberly, and in the fear of God.

One of the most naive aspects about many current "alternatives" to
marriage is their assumption that a vague feeling of "love" (ab-
stractly and vaguely defined) is enough to insure mutual trust and
consideration. The church has its doubts about the power of
romantic love alone to weather the storms of life. It insists that
couples pledge to stay together

> . . . this day forward, for better for worse, for richer for poorer, in sickness
> and in health, to love and to cherish, till death us do part. . . .

This gets us down to the hard, cold facts of life and demands that our
relationship confront those facts.

Considering the vicissitudes of life, changes within our personalities, and the unpredictability of the future, is it reasonable for
the church to ask a couple to risk this promise to lifelong

commitment? John Macquarrie, the great Anglican theologian, answers that question by referring to what it means to be a person— or become a person. One of the things which distinguishes humans from animals, according to Macquarrie, is our ability to look beyond the moment and pledge ourselves to commitments beyond the present. In matters great and small, we continually pledge ourselves beyond the moment. There could be no human community if we did not take certain promises and obligations upon ourselves and then faithfully keep them. Likewise, a person is shaped by his or her decisions and how he or she stands by them. Our abiding commitments make us who we are and give us unified characters in place of a tangled mass of loosely connected instincts, whims, and fads. Like the Christian faith itself, marriage requires basic commitment which is willing to endure times of stress, to renew and deepen itself over the years, and to grow and persevere together.[7]

The Christian marriage ceremony inherits the Christian faith's realism about who we are and who we are not. It knows that what we would do naturally is not always the best that we could do. We are, as Martin Luther taught us, a blend of saint and sinner, capable of alternation between selfishness and selflessness. That is why we demand things like marriage licenses, public ceremonies, and spoken vows. We expect a couple to say publicly what we trust they have said privately, "I will be with you no matter what happens." While Carl Rogers thinks, "The value of such outward commitment appears . . . to be just about nil,"[8] the church feels that a relationship needs a basis of something more firm than romantic love. *Hesed*—the biblical "steadfast love"—is needed.

The marriage vows are necessary because of our human nature and the nature of love. While it is true that "the law kills" and marriage which is based upon nothing but grim, dutiful legalism is a drab enterprise indeed, the unrestrained quest for personal fulfillment and individual freedom can just as quickly degenerate into a rationale for self-indulgence. The orderliness of God's world is not a straitjacket. It is our salvation. The underlying laws of the world are the source of our true happiness since they are related to who we really are and are created to be. While love may be one prerequisite for a good marriage, fidelity is also indispensable. As Emil Brunner has written:

> It is true, of course, that marriage springs from love, but its stability is based not on love but on fidelity. Fidelity is the ethical element which enhances natural love, and only by its means does the natural become

personal. It is therefore the only quality which can guarantee the permanence of the marriage relation. Through the marriage vows the feeling of love is absorbed into the personal will; this alone provides the guarantee to the other party which justifies the venture of such a life companionship.[9]

Mere keeping of one's marriage vows will not a marriage make. But without the kind of total, permanent, lifelong commitment that those vows represent, there is little possibility of a deep relationship. Fidelity, and the kind of sexual exclusiveness and total commitment that it represents, is out of fashion these days. But we must not discard something simply because it is difficult. For the theology of the Old Testament, for Jesus, and for Paul, marriage was most important as a symbol of faithfulness. This steadfast love and lifelong fidelity provide the context where true freedom and growth can occur. With the disappearance of the old cultural restraints and props for marriage, contemporary married couples must make deliberate, intentional, persevering efforts in order to achieve true union and must continually work to keep alive in themselves the vision of the kind of marriage they want.

While fidelity may begin as mere adherence to a vow, when that vow is kept, it soon becomes so much a part of us that our faithfulness feels natural. Marital research has documented the existence of certain peaks and valleys along the path of a marriage. For instance, a low point may occur when the children reach school age and again when the couple nears retirement age. Unfortunately, some couples mistake these natural low points in life as signs of marital disintegration and so dissolve their marriage.[10] Marriage affirms that life is the sum of all our moments, good and bad. The pride we feel when we have done a tough job together and have done it well and the joy of loving someone through thick and thin are the ultimate joys of a good marriage. While I do not wish to minimize the pain of living with a mate who has become mentally or physically disabled, who has been unfaithful, or cruel, or simply indifferent, I do wish to celebrate the nobility and sense of purpose among those who keep their commitments during such difficult circumstances. As I see it, "for better or worse . . ." in the marriage vows means, "I am willing to commit myself to you, with God as my helper, even when it is difficult, even when it requires self-sacrifice on my part, even when I have to forego some of my own pleasure in order to be with you. I promise to be there: forever."

Fidelity promises us that, if we will remain faithfully committed to the one we married, we will ultimately be more the recipient of love than the giver of love. As Robert Capon says: For those of us who spend half of our lives wishing we were somewhere else, with someone else, or (worse) wishing we were somebody else, there is grace in remaining with *these* children, *this* man or *this* woman, in *this* place.[11] It is the staying which enables us to experience the glory of the other person and our own glory as faithful, loving, caring persons—glory we might miss by not "hanging in there."

A few months ago, I was counseling with a couple before their marriage. I began, as I usually do, by taking them step by step through the *Service of Marriage* and explaining each part to them.

"My only problem with the service," the young man said, "is that it is too long. Could we shorten it?"

I told him that I was willing to consider modifications in the service but was surprised that he thought the service was too long. The service itself could not possibly take longer than a few minutes.

"What is it that you would like to omit from the service?" I asked.

"Well, for instance, all those old words about 'Will you love in sickness and health, richer and poorer,' etc. Why do we have to go through all that? Everybody who comes to the wedding knows how we feel about each other. Couldn't we just stand up there and say that we love one another and want to live together?"

"We may all know that you love each other," I replied. "But how do we know *how* you love each other? Is your problem with the length of the words or with what these words say?"

The young man looked puzzled.

I continued, "Love is a great thing. But we want to put some muscle into that sometimes flabby word. Sure, this woman beside you looks young, attractive, and lovable now. But what will you do with her when she is older, overweight, cantankerous, and not so easy to love? Is your present love for her willing to commit itself to the possibility of that kind of future with her?"

And then, looking at her, I asked, "What qualifications are you willing to set on this marriage? Would you be willing to live with him as long as you kept your weight down, or your politics stayed the same, or until you developed cancer or mental illness? What limitations would you be willing to accept on his commitment to you?"

What followed was a lively exchange, to say the least. The three of us were able to take a long, hard look at those ancient words in the marriage service and see them as a very contemporary challenge. Fortunately for herself and that young man, the bride-to-be wanted nothing less than total, lifelong, unqualified commitment from the man she was to marry and, for her part, was willing to commit as much to her mate. I do not know whether his desire to modify the service resulted from his eagerness to begin their honeymoon or from a tinge of cold feet at the thought of the radical promise he was about to make. I do know that, when the time came for them to stand together before the altar of God and the assembled congregation, they both displayed an air of firm commitment—as if they were undertaking some courageous, demanding act of revolutionary significance. And so they were!

"We love, because he first loved us," says John (1 John 4:19). God's love, as revealed to us in Jesus the Christ, has shown us the way to the most radical expression of human love. Christ totally committed himself to us, even to the point of suffering and death, even making us his very body (1 Corinthians 12:27; Ephesians 5:28-30). Even in our continuing unfaithfulness and unlovableness, he has loved us with a love that will not let us go. To see oneself as the object of that kind of self-giving, total, noncalculating, revolutionary, committed love is to feel oneself called to respond in love. We commit ourselves to one another, because he first committed himself to us.

Notes for Chapter 6

[1] Roy C. DeLamotte, "The Situational Wedding," *Today's Ministry* (May, 1974), pp. 79-81.

[2] Daniel Yankelovich, *The American Family Report: Raising Children in a Changing Society* (Minneapolis, Minn.: General Mills, Inc., 1977).

[3] "Family: New Breed v. the Old," *Time* (May 2, 1977), p. 76.

[4] Alvin Toffler, *Future Shock* (New York: Random House, 1970), pp. 47-67.

[5] Margaret Mead, "Ritual and Social Crisis," in James D. Shaughnessy, ed., *The Roots of Ritual* (Grand Rapids, Mich.: Wm. B. Eerdmans Publishing Co., 1973), p. 96.

[6] Philip E. Slater, *The Pursuit of Loneliness*, rev. ed (Boston: Beacon Press, 1970), pp. 135-138.

[7] John Macquarrie, "The Nature of the Marriage Bond," *Theology* (May, 1975), p. 233.

[8] Carl Rogers, *Becoming Partners: Marriage and Its Alternatives* (New York: Delacorte Press, 1972), p. 200.

[9] Emil Brunner, *The Divine Imperative,* trans. Olive Wyon (Philadelphia: The Westminster Press, 1947), pp. 357-358.

[10] Mary W. Hicks and Marilyn Platt, "Marital Happiness and Stability: A Review of the Research in the Sixties," *Journal of Marriage and the Family* (November, 1970), pp. 553-574.

[11] Robert Capon, *Bed and Board: Plain Talk About Marriage* (New York: Simon & Schuster, Inc., 1965), p. 155.

SONNET CXVI

William Shakespeare

Let me not to the marriage of true minds
Admit impediments. Love is not love
Which alters when it alteration finds,
Or bends with the remover to remove:
O no! it is an ever-fixèd mark
That looks on tempests, and is never shaken,
It is the star to every wandering bark,
Whose worth's unknown, although his height
    be taken.
Love's not Time's fool, though rosy lips
    and cheeks
Within his bending sickle's compass come;
Love alters not with his brief hours and
    weeks,
But bears it out even to the edge of doom.
    If this be error, and upon me proved,
    I never writ, nor no man ever loved.

7

The Subversiveness of Love

As a minister, when I do premarital counseling with a couple, one of the first questions I ask is whether or not they have been living together. About half of the ones I ask admit that they have. I ask this question not to pry unduly into their personal lives or as a prelude to a stern clerical lecture on the perils of "living in sin." I ask them this simply to state to them, at the beginning, that, as far as relationships go, there is as much difference between Christian marriage and the practice of simply "living together" as the difference between a Cadillac and a Toyota, as far as automobiles go. Having spoken of the risk of union and the challenge of commitment in Christian marriage, let us now speak of love.

In 1977, the U. S. Census Bureau estimated that some 1.3 million American adults were living together out of wedlock, double the number in 1970.[1] Presumably, most of these people felt that marriage was not a requisite for a loving relationship. In fact, many of them probably believed the widely held notion that marriage can inhibit or even ruin a good love relationship. As "couple counselor" (as opposed to "marriage counselor") Vincent Sweeney (who, after his divorce, moved in with Jane Donner, a divorced counselor) puts it, "Traditional marriage is a convenience to satisfy society or the law or the church. It doesn't have anything to do with people." At their Center for Study of Human Systems in affluent Chevy Chase, Maryland, Sweeney and Donner help people achieve "better communication and intimacy" through their extramarital relationships.[2] There are many others who live together, not so much to avoid marriage but rather to test themselves in a kind of "trial run" arrangement to see if they are suited for marriage.

Contrary to contemporary popular folk wisdom, such premarital trial runs are not always reliable. After reviewing the research into these premarital arrangements, Delia Ephron concluded, "If a couple has lived together happily before marriage, they have proved something: They can live together happily before marriage."[3] That is all. She cites a family therapist at New York's Nathan W. Ackerman Institute who says, "No matter how long a couple has lived together, if they get married, it's a whole new ball game."[4] The problem is that marriage cannot be simulated. Some researchers have hypothesized that one reason "living together" is unlike marriage is that marriage makes a relative out of a lover! It is one thing to live with someone in a relatively casual, short-term encounter. A formal, committed, sexually exclusive, lifetime union is something else. In short, marriage—seen from the perspective of today's values—is too close for comfort. I can think of no greater compliment to marriage than that!

Marriage is out of favor with many people these days partly because the word "love" has been emptied of significance. "Love" has been commercialized, sentimentalized, and prostituted in the service of everything from advertising to pornography. "Love" has become abstracted and disjointed from the concrete realities of everyday life. We will not understand Christian marriage until we first understand the radical nature of Christian love. Toward that aim, I would like to offer a modest definition of Christian love, particularly as it relates to marriage: Christian love, as manifested in marriage, is an *expression of an enduring, total commitment to unite with another person, which reflects God's union with us through Christ.*

First of all, the love of which I speak endures. It ". . . bears all things, believes all things, hopes all things, endures all things" (1 Corinthians 13:7). As we said in the last chapter, it is love which is permanently committed to the other person. The great theologian Karl Barth has said that the love of Christian marriage is love in its most mature and Christlike manifestation. Just as God has freely yoked himself to us and graciously covenanted himself with us and for us in a permanent relationship that transcends changes of time and circumstance, so marriage is meant to be the human equivalent of this divine covenant.[5] Love is best in marriage because in the context of promised permanence and fidelity, love is truly free.

Many couples report that the worst period in their relationship is the engagement. During this time, in each person's mind are questions about the rightness of the marriage, the depth of their affection for one another, their ability to grow together, etc. In this setting, there is always the possibility that each argument will be the last, that when the other person walks out and slams the door in a huff, he or she will not come back. Marriage should change all this because, once permanence is promised, each person is free to be his or her real self. There is no longer a need for the games, the masks, the little falsehoods. Now your arguments can be more honest and more productive, your lovemaking more carefree and uninhibited, your sharing of yourself more revealing. The one with whom you argue and make love and expose your innermost self is the one who has covenanted to be with you forever.

As Barth said in another context, no one can truly repent or dare to be truly honest about his shortcomings and sins unless he is first absolutely convinced of the security and permanence of God's love. The best Christian theology proclaims grace before it preaches judgment because it knows that unless we first accept grace, we will never willingly receive judgment. Any repentance and confession before this is just playacting. What is true of the divine-human relationship is true of the human relationship of marriage. The covenanting of two people in marriage brings a sense of security and openness that is found almost nowhere else in human encounters. Only in this long-term relationship can the honesty, forgiveness, acceptance, and healing take place that make life together possible.

The shallow, gushy "love" of our contemporary world is pagan love that loves only the lovely and the lovable. It is the love of the white person who loves black people only when they conform to white expectations and the love of rich people who have sympathy for poor people only when they are the "deserving poor." It loves "humanity" in the abstract and "mankind" in some idealized form but is repulsed by the concrete actualities of particular men and women. It loves the neighbor as long as he or she is across town and not next door. It leaves baskets of food on needy doorsteps while we are filled with Christmas spirit but quibbles and gripes all year long over Food Stamp "giveaways." It is bad enough when such selfish, on-again off-again affection passes for love in our society, but it is disaster when it is applied to a marriage. David Head has captured the vapidity of this "love" in his satirical marriage prayer of the "natural man":

May we find marriage the end of all our problems, and live happily ever after. May he have no secrets, and never discover mine. May she be always useful and always beautiful, full of interesting conversation, witty in private and sparkling in public, blind to my faults, tolerant with my follies, never weary, never demanding, enjoying her own company when necessary, not getting too involved with female friends, performing miracles with her house-keeping allowance, and always grateful that I married her.[6]

These naive marital expectations, unimaginative definitions of love, and shifting affections make a poor foundation for marital fidelity. Add to this situation our American uprootedness, mobility, and material competitiveness and you will know why marriage is on hard times. There is no freedom for honesty or growth where people feel they are potentially disposable, expandable, and subject to the fickle whims of the moment. "Our highest moral principle is flexibility," observes Roman Catholic philosopher Michael Novak. Many of us believe that

. . . life is solitary and brief, and that its aim is self-fulfillment. In such a vision of the self, marriage is merely an alliance. . . . They say of marriage that it is deadening, when what they mean is that it drives us beyond adolescent fantasies and romantic dreams. . . . Choosing to have a family used to be uninteresting. It is, today, an act of intelligence and courage.[7]

Christian love, as manifested in marriage, has become in our time a countercultural, subversive activity: Christian love is enduring, totally committed love.

But perhaps the major difference between our pagan definitions of love and Christian love is that Christian love is more than a feeling. Romantic love and married love, while having a certain connection with one another, nevertheless are quite different. As the late Dr. Carl Michalson once wrote:

Romantic love is irresponsible love, uncommitted love. That is why it is such fun! Married love is committed love, responsible love. That is why it is so mature! But if you ask marriage to sustain the same conditions of love that are present in courtship, you put a strain on it. For this reason the church takes a very dim view of extra-marital sex relations. The sex act implies childbirth, and childbirth implies responsibility. . . . The sex act outside marriage, outside committed love, outside responsible love, is a contradiction in terms. Now it is true that love and marriage go together like a horse and carriage, but when the love of courtship is hitched to the carriage of marriage, it becomes a horse of a different color.[8]

Romantic love is full of feeling. And feelings are fine, as far as they go. But feelings are also notoriously fickle. Passion, infatuation, and heartwarming affections are delightful human experiences, but they are not a durable enough foundation for marriage—or for any other significant work of love. Any significant work takes time. And time is the greatest enemy of feelings and romantic attachments. Passion is notoriously short-lived. Therefore I have some sympathy with the character in Dryden's Song from "Marriage à la Mode" who complains:

> Why should a foolish marriage vow,
>   Which long ago was made,
> Oblige us to each other now,
>   When passion is decayed?
> We loved, and we loved, as long as we could,
>   Till our love was loved out in us both;
> But our marriage is dead when the pleasure is fled:
>   'Twas pleasure first made it an oath.[9]

As many in our own time have found, marriage built on passion and pleasure alone makes vows foolish and union doomed to failure. Marriage needs a more substantial foundation.

Christian marriage affirms that love is more than a feeling; it is a conscious decision to yoke oneself with another person through thick and thin ("sickness and health, etc. . . ."). In the marriage ritual the minister asks not, "Do you love this person?" The minister, on behalf of the church, asks, "*Will* you love this person?" The faith assumes that loving is something one can decide to do. We can will to love. The basis for marriage is not so much a feeling but rather a promise. I have sometimes reminded couples who come to me to discuss divorce because "we don't love each other anymore" that once they stood before God and the church and *promised* to love. Unlike those "brute beasts that have no understanding" which the *Book of Common Prayer* used to warn couples about, one thing that makes us human is our ability to decide, to promise, and to live by our promises.

Throughout the entire marriage ceremony, there is a surprising lack of attention to feelings and emotions, not even much talk about love. Rather, the service is filled with vows, promises, duties, and obligations. This again illustrates the peculiar nature of Christian love. Alexander Magoun has contrasted Christian love with romantic infatuation through the following analogy: Romantic love is like a tourist who visits a foreign country for his own edification and enjoyment. The sights, information, and possessions which he accumulates are the sum total of his experience there. The person who is truly in love is more accurately compared to a member of the

Peace Corps who decides to spend time abroad to benefit the local population. His primary purpose is to give rather than to receive. Yet, paradoxically, he will probably end up seeing more, learning more, and acquiring more than the casual tourist. "In giving you receive." In committing ourselves to self-giving love, it is true love which we receive in return.

Married love is based on a decision, a conscious act of the will, to be in union with another person: totally, permanently, unqualifiedly.

Finally, we are bold to claim that human love in marriage is, in spite of its many shortcomings and problems, a reflection of God's own love. The Bible is the long story of how that divine love sought us out, called us, chose us, endured us, forgave us, and continues to love us even in our continuing unfaithfulness, even when we are most unlovable. God's love is always seeking, giving, promising. In the midst of Israel's idolatrous unfaithfulness, Hosea hears the Lord say:

> ". . . I will betroth you to me forever; I will betroth you to me in righteousness and justice, in steadfast love, and in mercy. I will betroth you to me in faithfulness; and you shall know the Lord" (Hosea 2:19-20).

In God's dealings with us, we see the manner in which he wishes us to deal with one another. "We love, because he first loved us."

Vows, duties, equality, and mutuality in marriage are necessary. But, in the end, even our most noble definitions of mutual submission and reasonable responsibility do not go far enough. In the end, only love will do. As a theologian, Reinhold Niebuhr affirmed the necessity for just structures in society, equality in law, and fairness in our economic systems. But when it came to marriage, Niebuhr recognized that even so noble an ideal as justice would not go far enough:

> Family life is too intimate to be preserved by the spirit of justice. It can only be sustained by a spirit of love, which goes beyond justice. Justice requires that we carefully weigh rights and privileges and assure that each member of a community receive his due share. Love does not weigh rights and privileges too carefully because it prompts each to bear the burden of the other.[10]

Only self-giving, sacrificial, noncalculating love is equal to the task of living in the close physical, emotional, and spiritual proximity of marriage. As long as we hold some part of ourselves back, quibble over our respective rights and privileges, or look upon our marriage as only a vow and not a vocation, we will be forever tiptoeing about the perimeters of what could be the most significant relationship of our lives. As Paul Scherer, Niebuhr's colleague at Union Seminary, put it, "Love is a spendthrift, leaves its arithmetic at home, is always 'in the red.'"[11]

The greatest gift one human being can give another is the gift of love and acceptance. And it is a gift. It is something that each one of us can give someone else, no matter who we are. In marriage, love cannot be earned or deserved. None of us is worthy of receiving such total commitment from another person. It only comes as a gift. The Christian faith has traditionally described it as "grace." It is the miracle of receiving something which you did not and cannot earn or work for, even as we have received the love of God. The gift of love leads to the freedom to love in return, for it is necessary for us to have the security of acceptance and love in order that we return acceptance and love. Love changes us, gives us new beings, subverts our old standards of responsibility, surprises us with our own ability to respond to the challenge of love. There is no greater gift to give or receive.

One of the three purposes of marriage as set forth in the *Book of Common Prayer* (the other two being "procreation of children" and "to avoid fornication") is "for the mutual society, help, and comfort, that one ought to have of the other, both in prosperity and adversity." While Martin Luther stayed firmly in the tradition of Augustine and Aquinas before him, seeing woman's function as primarily a childbearer, man as primarily a domestic master, and marriage primarily for the relief of concupiscence, John Calvin stressed, as we have in this study, the relational aspects of marriage. Woman was seen by Calvin as a companion and marriage was emphasized as a social rather than a generative relationship.[12] At its best, Protestantism in the twentieth century has dealt with sex in a more intrinsic and relational nature going beyond traditional preoccupation with procreation. It is time for us to deal with marriage in a similar way, as an institution with implications for society as a whole.

As stated earlier, the uniting of two people in marriage is a paradigm of the manner of life that God intends, not only for these two people but also for the world as a whole. Admittedly the history of relations between the sexes tells us that there have long been "alternatives" to marriage and few marriages have attained the ideal of a committed, permanent, unqualified union. While there is much about our modern mores that makes this an especially difficult time for love, for that very reason this is a special time for married Christians. Marriage, in an age of pagan love and lonely disunity, has taken on a missionary character. Marriage has come of age. Contrary to the tradition which regarded marriage as little more than a setting for human reproduction to occur, many of the Reformers recovered the vision of marriage as vocation, as discipleship. Marriage is vocation in the sense that it is a call to a manner of life that is demanding and difficult but possible through God's help. Marriage is discipleship in that it requires disciplined, intentional commitment which rises above individual weaknesses, present problems, and selfish concerns.

> "A new commandment I give to you, that you love one another; even as I have loved you, that you also love one another. By this all men will know that you are my disciples, if you have love for one another" (John 13:34-35).

In today's world, marriage has become a witness to the world that it is possible for people to live together, in love and mutual respect, for a lifetime. Amid the world's bad news marriage has become an evangelistic word of good news: that union is possible, that loneliness and isolation are not our only human options, that the establishment values of "do you own thing" and "look out for number one" may have it all wrong.

I remember the comedienne Lily Tomlin asking somewhere, with a touch of pathos in her voice, "If love is the answer, would someone please restate the question?" My colleague at Duke, Dr. Charles Robinson, attempted to answer Miss Tomlin in a recent sermon that went something like this: The question is, How amid this difficult, sad, tragic world can our lives be lived with meaning? The answer is love. That is the only answer. Not because it is expected, or because it is the popular thing to do, or by our human nature we are inclined to do it, but because we are called by the Giver of Life to love—even as we have been loved by him. Otherwise, there is no meaning to it all, no purpose behind our enduring and suffering with and for others, no reason to be with others beyond the passing of the moment. "For I am sure," says Paul in his letter to the Romans, "that neither death, nor life, nor angels, nor principalities, nor things present, nor things to come, nor powers, nor height, nor depth, nor anything else in all creation, will separate us from the love of God in Christ Jesus our Lord" (Romans 8:38-39). *Nothing* can separate us! What power, what comfort, what challenge in these thundering words! Our love in marriage is not some heroic effort of self-sacrifice. It is merely a response to that loving unity which we have experienced in Christ. Our love has meaning because of our belief that this love reflects the very nature of reality itself; it is congruent with the order of the universe; it is our created destiny. This love is the only thing that will finally enable us to hear, even amid the jarring, jangling, discordant cacophony of life's inevitable tragedy and misfortune, a final symphony being played, a pattern that ultimately fits together, a union that brings forth new life. Love is the only answer.

Marriage will probably continue to be unpopular, and people will probably continue to search for "alternatives." As we have suggested, many people's dissatisfaction with marriage may be related to the fact that it is difficult and demanding, calling forth the best that we have. The values of marriage challenge many of the values we have accepted over the past few years. In a world of flux where everything and everyone seems to have a price, where few dare to link themselves with other people for a moment much less a lifetime, where television tells us we can have anything we want with no risk and have it right now, where people are used, and abused, and disposed of as easily as returnable soft-drink cans, marriage has become a revolutionary, downright subversive activity!

As revolutionary as the love of Christ himself!

Notes for Chapter 7

[1] Cited by Daniel St. Albin Green, "'Living in Sin' Is in Style," *The National Observer* (May 30, 1977), p. 1.

[2] *Ibid.*, p. 16.

[3] Delia Ephron, "The State of the Union: New Scientific Facts About Marriage," *Esquire* (February, 1977), p. 64.

[4] *Ibid.*

[5] Karl Barth, *Church Dogmatics, The Doctrine of Creation,* ed. G. W. Bromiley and T. F. Torrance (Edinburgh: T. & T. Clark, 1961), vol. 3, part 4, pp. 196f.

[6] David Head, *He Sent Leanness* (New York: Macmillan, Inc., 1959), pp. 42-43.

[7] Quoted in *Time*, "The New Housewife Blues" (March 14, 1977), p. 70.

[8] Carl Michalson, *The Witness of Radical Faith,* ed. Gordon E. Michalson and Olin M. Ivey (Nashville, Tenn.: Tidings, 1974), pp. 101-102. Used by permission of Discipleship Resources, P.O. Box 840, Nashville, TN 37202.

[9] John Dryden, Song from "Marriage à la Mode" in *The Norton Anthology of English Literature*, vol. 1, rev. ed., ed. M. H. Abrams, *et al.* (New York: W. W. Norton & Company, Inc., 1968), p. 1358.

[10] Reinhold Niebuhr, quoted in *The Rosicrucian Digest* (July, 1974), p. 13.

[11] Paul Scherer, *Love Is a Spendthrift* (New York: Harper & Row, Publishers, 1961), p. 15.

[12] Jacob Dominian, *Christian Marriage: The Challenge of Change* (London: Darton, Longman & Todd Ltd., 1968), p. 83.

A Pastoral Postscript:
Divorce

I cannot leave the subject of Christian marriage without a word on divorce. As you have read the preceding pages on marriage, I am sure that the subject of marital breakdown was in the back of your mind. Behind the foregoing affirmation of marriage stands the specter of an increasing number of marriages that do not hold together, do not succeed, do not produce sought-for happiness, and so they are dissolved. There are three times as many divorces in America today as in 1900.[1] Divorce is a reality we must face, and we must face it with something more than a loud defensive polemic in behalf of marriage. While I am willing to let stand all that I have affirmed about marriage, my pastoral sensitivities remind me that there are many fine people for whom marriage has been a spiritual and emotional disaster. The church's good intentions in regard to marriage have resulted in bad dealings in regard to divorce. In legalistic, pharisaic fashion we have taught that divorce is wrong and to be avoided at all costs. In the midst of our vehement denunciations of divorce we have expended too little effort in improving marriage, preparing people for marriage, and supporting people in the midst of marital difficulties. We in the church must admit to the hypocrisy of condemning divorce while at the same time condoning as marriage the state of those in our midst for whom "marriage" is little more than a cynical armistice in which two people have settled down into mutual boredom, suppressed hostility, or legalized prostitution. Too often we have been blind to the difficulties in marriage, treated divorced persons as if they were modern lepers, and in general approached the

87

entire subject with an attitude of "nice people like us don't do things like divorce."

But more and more "nice people" are getting divorced. If, as we have said in this book, marriage is a creative, courageous, demanding, risky act, then it must also carry with it the possibility of failure. That failure is called divorce. It is a tough failure to live through. A number of sociological and psychological studies have shown that the majority of spouses involved in divorce endure a high rate of emotional stress, greater than being sentenced to a jail term and far greater than the shock of the death of a close relative. Divorced people have a higher mortality rate and are statistically more subject to emotional and physical disorders than other people. In his *Divorced in America*, Joseph Epstein claims that, "In divorce there are only smaller and larger disasters." [2]

In spite of the data on the trauma of divorce, there are those who contend that, far from being an unmitigated evil, divorce can be a positive good. Dr. Frank Sommers, a Toronto psychiatrist, sees the rising divorce rate as a sign of new growth among people: "It's overdue. People are stepping out into life again to grow as individuals. They are awakening to their own human potential. They want more out of life than food and shelter." [3] Many have come to view divorce as a natural consequence of personal growth and the attainment of selfhood. Instead of considering divorce as a failure, the authors of *The Courage to Divorce* put the shoe on the other foot and argue that "all married couples should be considered dependent, neurotic, and too fearful to divorce." They ridicule the analogy between divorce and death. "Why should people want to mourn the 'loss' of someone they prefer to be rid of or have outgrown?" [4]

The logic in these new attempts to defend divorce is as fuzzy as that in some of the old attempts to condemn divorce. More complex and more important human questions are at stake here than some of this pro and con rhetoric would have us believe. Having examined the nature of marriage, let us now look at the nature of divorce, taking as our starting point the beliefs about divorce in the Bible.

In spite of Malachi's word from the Lord, ". . . I hate divorce" (Malachi 2:16a), in the Old Testament divorce was generally permitted, on the initiative of the husband, without stigma or litigation:

> When a man hath taken a wife, and married her, and it come to pass that she find no favour in his eyes, because he hath found some uncleanness in

her: then let him write her a bill of divorcement, and give it in her hand, and send her out of his house (Deuteronomy 24:1, KJV).

The definition of "some uncleanness in her" was rather loosely defined in the Old Testament. Some viewed this as applying only to acts of adultery (see Matthew 1:19f.); some permitted divorce for religious reasons (Ezra 10:3, 44) or childlessness (Malachi 2:15).[5] Some rabbis even allowed a man to divorce his wife on the basis of her bad cooking! This obviously led to abuses of divorce and made a woman's position extremely vulnerable.

For Jesus it was different:

> And Pharisees came up to him and tested him by asking, "Is it lawful to divorce one's wife for any cause?" He answered, "Have you not read that he who made them from the beginning made them male and female, and said, 'For this reason a man shall leave his father and mother and be joined to his wife, and the two shall become one flesh'? So they are no longer two but one flesh. What therefore God has joined together, let no man put asunder." They said to him, "Why then did Moses command one to give a certificate of divorce, and to put her away?" He said to them, "For your hardness of heart Moses allowed you to divorce your wives, but from the beginning it was not so. And I say to you: Whoever divorces his wife, except for unchastity, and marries another, commits adultery" (Matthew 19:3-9).

Mark 10:11-12 and Luke 16:18 clearly show Jesus taking a hard stand against divorce. In Mark 10:11-12, Jesus says,

> "Whoever divorces his wife and marries another, commits adultery against her; and if she divorces her husband and marries another, she commits adultery."

The later version in Matthew 5:32 seems to soften Jesus' attitude to allow for the extenuating circumstances of adultery,

> ". . . every one who divorces his wife, except on the ground of unchastity, makes her an adulteress; and whoever marries a divorced woman commits adultery."

Paul, while simply repeating what he must have regarded as an important and authentic saying of Jesus against divorce, adds another extenuating circumstance: if one is married to an unbeliever who demands a divorce, then one may remarry (1 Corinthians 7:15).

The biblical evidence indicates that Jesus categorically forbids divorce and remarriage after divorce and bases his prohibition on an appeal to God's original intention in creation (". . . from the beginning it was not so.") by quoting Genesis 2:24. Divorce is not a part of God's intended scheme of things. Remarriage after divorce is called "adultery," one of the most heinous sins in Mosaic law. These are hard sayings of Jesus. Some speculate that Jesus' real concern was over the abuse of divorce and its attendant victimization of women rather than a condemnation of divorce itself.[6] While Jesus would definitely disapprove of the way women were treated in the patriarchal divorce system, there is no way to sidestep the fact that Jesus condemned divorce using the strongest possible words. His words on divorce are hard sayings indeed.

But the biblical evidence also tells us that the early church, after stating the unequivocal demand of Jesus, felt free to permit exceptions to his words on divorce. Matthew 19:9; 5:32; and 1 Corinthians 7:15 are examples of this attempt by the church, in its earliest days, to deal humanely with actual situations of marriage problems while still upholding Jesus' demand. There is no denying that Christian ethics have always been somewhat situational long before Joseph Fletcher's *Situational Ethics* (1966). Situational ethics differs from code morality in that code morality stresses laws, mandates, and inflexible codes of behavior. Jesus criticized the Pharisees for their elaborate and rigid codes of morality which sometimes stood in the way of truly moral actions. On the other hand, situationalists, while accepting the validity of laws and rules, refuse to make laws and rules binding and absolute on all people at all times and places. For the situationalist, the only absolute is the Great Commandment (Matthew 22:37-40). The situationalist says that we Christians are called to seek the most loving action possible within the context of a given situation. That action might include reference to an inherited moral code, but it might deviate from the code in order that the supreme command to love might be honored. Love takes precedence over other values. Situationalists cite Jesus' own actions, such as the healing (Mark 3:1-6) and the gleaning (Mark 2:23-28) on the sabbath to show that Jesus put love first.

From the situationalist stance, Robert Sinks argues that there can be no absolute, universally binding law prohibiting Christians from divorce. There are times, according to Sinks, when even divorce may be appropriate in order to fulfill the law of love:

> If Jesus allowed for breaking the honored Sabbath laws so as to provide for healing or gleaning, though ancient laws forbade these on the sacred day, would he not also allow for a suspension of the proscription against divorce if such were to liberate a person from the bondage of an intolerable

marriage? If the Sabbath was "made for man, not man for the Sabbath" (Mark 2:27), does it not follow that marriage was made for humanity, rather than humanity for marriage? If the institution, important as it is, does violence to the individual, then shouldn't the institution be amended in order that the individual might flourish?[7]

While Sinks admits that some divorces are clearly acts arising from sinful and selfish motives, he claims that other divorces, while resulting from the evil, fallen nature of humanity and the world, are not specifically sinful acts. Divorce can be a responsible decision reached in the context of tragic, painful, limited circumstances. The question Sinks would have people in situations of marital stress to ask is:

"Which—among the choices realistically available—is the least evil?" or "What is the best alternative in hand?" The issue is not whether divorce is hurtful or a result of sin. It is usually both. The focal question is this: among the available options (desertion, separation, divorce, homicide, suicide, continuation of the marriage), which is the best and most humane solution? The situationist recognizes that divorce, painful as it is, may well be the least harmful option in some situations, and thus it may best fulfill the Great Commandment.[8]

The situationalist approach does have the advantage of moving us away from rigid legalism while still demanding careful consideration of the marital situation and its relationship to the demands of the faith.

The weakness of the situationalist approach, when it is applied to divorce or any other ethical issue, is that it eschews rules and codes in favor of the rather broad, unspecific, vague code of "love." Is love alone a sufficient basis for our ethics? What about other moral values, such as selflessness, commitment, justice, sacrifice, honesty, fidelity, etc.? Might not "love" be perverted into a congenial moral umbrella which is used to cover and condone all our actions, regardless of their ends and means? Can we so quickly dispose of the moral principles behind Jesus' prohibition of divorce without considering the source and the goal of those principles? We moderns have a disagreeable tendency to rebel against any law or rule as an unnatural limitation of our freedom and to justify our actions on psychological or utilitarian grounds. Can we afford to trust ourselves (and others) to let the situation determine the validity of a given moral principle? I fear that, in our admirable desire to deal with divorced and divorcing persons in a more humane way, we have offered them cheap grace in place of the gospel, vague and permissive generalities in place of an honest confrontation with the challenge of marriage and the tragedy of divorce.

When Christians today, hearing the "hard sayings" of Jesus, affirm Jesus' prohibition of divorce, we are not upholding an impossible, perfectionist ideal, an unrealistic interim ethic, or a hardhearted legalistic command. Jesus' sayings about divorce and marriage are grounded in his perception of God's original intention in creation. "The two shall be one flesh." The whole creation, as Paul put it, groans together awaiting union. Separation is sin, not because some law says so, but because it is a violation of the inherent order of things. We have here not a command but an invitation to participate, through our marital unions, with the underlying unifying purpose of all creation. The prohibition against divorce is not a regulation but a call to be free to be who we are created to be. While admitting to the possibility of divorce as the best thing to do in certain tragic situations, we must also sound an honest warning to those who contemplate or choose divorce. Having been honest about the risks involved in marriage, it may be time for the church to lead the way in being honest about the risks involved in divorce. Our disapproval of divorce is based more on practicality than prudishness. Divorce, we believe, goes against the nature of things.

At the risk of being too philosophical, I would warn against divorce by an appeal to the nature of time and of human relationships in time.[9] Aquinas once wrote that even our omnipotent God shares one limitation with us humans, "God cannot make what is past not to have been."[10] Time is not cyclic nor is it illusory. Time is real. The past is behind us, the present is the time for action, the future is determined by our deeds today. Jesus' message on forgiveness is not that it doesn't matter what we did. His message is that the future is not utterly determined by the past, and that, through repentance and conversion, even now we can relate to God.

If it were true that our past does not matter, as our modern neophiliac and permissive society constantly tells us, then the future does not matter either. Nor does the present matter or any of our actions at any time. I am not yet ready to admit to that brand of despair. Our deeds do count for something. Past facts of our lives cannot be altered or ignored. We are the sum total of all that we have been: past deeds, past promises, past loves, Even God cannot wipe away the past.

There are some human relationships that are adequately fulfilled in one action, such as a business deal. Something is promised and something is given and it is over. Marriage is a human relationship which is unlimited either by circumstance or lapse of time, "so long as ye both shall live." The shared joys and sorrows, the mutual secrets and hopes, the contract of marriage and the union it effects have profound and continuing significance. There is no such person as an "ex-wife" or an "ex-father." Certain actions are unalterably significant. What is done is done forever. You may be estranged, but you will never again be a stranger. We can never be entirely independent, completely on our own, totally free from a union once promised and participated in. That is why it is not helpful to quibble over questions of whether a given marriage is a "real" or "valid" marriage in the first place. If vows were exchanged in freedom, and the intention to unite was once there, then there has been a marriage, however unsatisfactory that marriage may have been. There was meeting and union. A promise was made and promises can be broken, but they can never be retrieved. Such irrevocable deeds may be regretted or repented, but they cannot be undone. There will be that old familiar feeling which crops up on occasions, that wistful longing that drifts in unexpectedly, that pain that continues from the unhealed wounds, that persistent personality trait that led you to make the marriage vow in the first place.

Those whose marriages have broken down can experience forgiveness and new beginnings, but only if they first recognize the reality of what has been done and its continuing significance for their situation. In my own pastoral counseling experiences, I have found that most divorcing couples are realistic enough not to want superficial, cheap attempts on our part to heal their wounds lightly by telling them, in effect, that their divorce is not all that important. For to tell them this is to imply that all of their life's deeds, promises, and loves are unimportant. There will be no future healing if the couple deludes itself, through our misguided attempts to provide loving support, into thinking that their divorce is a momentary inconvenience which is best forgotten rather than a broken relationship which will exert continuing influence upon their lives. As Henri Nouwen says, ". . . to forget our sins may be an even greater sin than to commit them. Why? Because what is forgotten cannot be healed and that which cannot be healed easily becomes the cause of greater evil." [11] We cannot face God unless we first face these facts of our lives which are inherently unalterable and which will be of continuing relevance to us. "One flesh" is an empirical, experiential reality.

Helen Oppenheimer has spoken of the inherently unnatural, painful nature of divorce:

> . . . a broken marriage is a broken marriage; something that stands out as an unnatural smashing of what was built to last, a blasphemy against the unity of Christ and his Church, an amputation inflicted upon a living body. . . . The bond of marriage is indeed a real bond, affecting those who are joined in it for evermore. It can never be neatly untied, only harshly severed. When this injury has happened the practical question is how the wound can best be healed, and the temptation is always either to cover it soothingly up at grave risk of its festering, or to keep it open for ever as a warning to others . . . even grave injuries can sometimes be healed. . . .[12]

I have always regarded "a friendly divorce" as an emotional nonsequitur. There is something vaguely immoral about two people sharing everything they have, joining together in wedlock, beginning a home, and then one day, politely shaking hands and amicably going separate ways. I am not pleading for judgment against divorced persons or for a "hard line" on divorce. I am pleading for simple honesty. Let us be honest about divorce, viewing it only as a painful last resort, rarely "good" or "right" in the eyes of God. Divorce is not a satisfactory course of action for times when marriage gets difficult, when love is being tested, or when vows are hard to keep. Marriage can be very difficult, but so can divorce. Divorce is a sign of failure, a sign that a meeting failed, a union was severed. Divorce is a sign of the presence of evil, a sign that love was overcome, a promise was not kept. Our word of grace to divorced persons must be that such failure and evil would destroy us were it not for the fact that God keeps his promises and continues his love even when we break our promises and our love fails. The past cannot be erased, but it can be forgiven. Life's painful actions of "last resort" can be done, not by rationalizing away the difficulties of the moral situation, but by firmly relying on the grace of God. "Love God and sin boldly," Luther says.

The practical pastoral burden upon pastors and parishioners in dealing with divorce is to be bold in holding to the will of God as we see it expressed in marriage and at the same time boldly loving our brothers and sisters who are in the throes of divorce. There will always be a note of judgment in the church's dealings with divorce. If it is not there, we are being dishonest and unfaithful. But let it be judgment like that of the Old Testament prophets who could be painfully honest with Israel over her failures to live up to her covenant with God and at the same time could be moved to sympathetic tears over her plight in her infidelity. If this seems logically and ethically inconsistent, do not be troubled. We Christians are called, not to consistency, but to faith, hope, and love. Faithfulness necessitates judgment. Love always requires grace.

While Saint Augustine did not know everything about love, sex, and marriage, and much of what he wrote on these subjects is less than helpful, Augustine did know a great deal about the grace of God. He knew that our noblest attempts to do good are doomed to failure unless we rely on God's grace to aid us. He knew that our great failures to do good will utterly crush us unless we rely upon the grace of God to forgive and sustain us. I think the saint's words to those of us in marriage and in divorce today might be the same as those he addressed to the struggling Christians of his own day:

> God therefore does not command impossibilities, but in His command He counsels you both to do what you can for yourself, and to seek His aid in what you cannot do.[13]

Notes for the Postscript

[1] Hugh Carter and Paul C. Glick, *Marriage and Divorce: A Social and Economic Study* (Cambridge: Harvard University Press, 1970), p. 387.

[2] Joseph Epstein, *Divorced in America: Marriage in an Age of Possibility* (New York: E. P. Dutton & Co., 1974), p. 256.

[3] Quoted by Paul Nowack in "Till Divorce Do Us Part," *Maclean's* (April 19, 1976), pp. 26-31.

[4] Susan Gettleman and Janet Markowitz, *The Courage to Divorce* (New York: Simon & Schuster, Inc., 1974).

[5] O. J. Baab, "Divorce," *The Interpreter's Dictionary of the Bible,* ed. G. A. Buttrick (Nashville: Abingdon Press, 1962), vol. 1, p. 859.

[6] Robert F. Sinks, "A Theology of Divorce," *The Christian Century* (April 20, 1977), p. 376.

[7] *Ibid.*, pp. 377-378.

[8] *Ibid.*, p. 378.

[9] I am indebted to J. R. Lucas's article, "The 'Vinculum Conjugale': A Moral Reality," _Theology_ (May, 1975), pp. 226-230 for the preceding thoughts on divorce.

[10] _Ibid._, p. 226.

[11] Henri J. M. Nouwen, _The Living Reminder_ (New York: The Seabury Press, Inc., 1977), p. 17.

[12] Helen Oppenheimer, "Is the Marriage Bond an Indissoluble 'Vinculum'?" _Theology_ (May, 1975), p. 242.

[13] _Saint Augustin: Anti-Pelagian Writings,_ in _Nicene and Post-Nicene Fathers_, ed. Philip Schaff (New York: Charles Scribner's Sons, 1902), vol. 5, p. 138.